EVANGELIZING AMERICA

Edited by
Thomas P. Rausch, S.J.

Paulist Press
New York/Mahwah, N.J.

Cover design by Diego Linares
Book design by Lynn Else

Library of Congress Cataloging-in-Publication Data

Evangelizing America / edited by Thomas P. Rausch.
   p.   cm.
  Includes bibliographical references.
  ISBN 0-8091-4240-6 (alk. paper)
  1. Catholic Church—United States. 2. Evangelistic work—United States. 3. Evangelistic work—Catholic Church. I. Rausch, Thomas P.

BX1406.3.E93 2004
266'.273—dc22

                                      2003028126

Published by Paulist Press
997 Macarthur Boulevard
Mahwah, New Jersey 07430

www.paulistpress.com

Printed and bound in the
United States of America

Contents

Contents

Acknowledgments

To all those who made this book possible, I am grateful. Three of the chapters were presented as papers at the annual meeting of the Catholic Theological Society of America in Milwaukee, Wisconsin, in 2001. Cardinal Avery Dulles's chapter is a revised version of a lecture he gave for the Intercultural Forum at the Pope John Paul II Cultural Center in Washington, D.C., on November 13, 2001. I'm grateful to Father J. Augustine Di Noia, O.P., then director of the center, for letting me use Cardinal Dulles's address. And to my graduate assistant, Ryan Ignatius Pratt, for his help in preparing the manuscript.

Finally, I would like to express my appreciation and gratitude to each of the contributors. My hope is that this book will help move all Christians to a greater appreciation of the church's evangelical mission in all its richness.

Thomas P. Rausch, S.J.

For Cardinal Avery Dulles, S.J.

Introduction

How can the church carry out its evangelical mission more effectively in a world that is at once both religiously pluralistic and increasingly secular? While this is a challenge for all the churches today, for Roman Catholics, it raises both particular questions and unique opportunities.

The question is challenging first of all because many Catholics today are not comfortable with the language of evangelization. As Avery Dulles, now Cardinal Dulles, has noted, if fifty years ago someone had asked the question: "Can the Roman Catholic Church be evangelical," some Catholics and practically all Evangelicals would have answered with a "no." Protestant churches, he explains, "could be churches of proclamation and evangelization, but the Catholic Church was a church of liturgy and law, centered on tradition, hierarchy, and sacraments."[1] In contemporary Roman Catholicism, in spite of the church's long commitment to missionary work, such work has been seen as a special vocation, not as a task of the whole church.

At the same time, the Roman Catholic Church has some unique resources for a revitalized evangelical mission in the contemporary world. First, its tradition of evangelization is in many ways both older and richer than that of Evangelical Protestantism. While the church has been oriented toward mission from its beginning, from the sixteenth century on the post-Reformation Catholic Church has been heavily committed to bringing the gospel to the

---

1. Avery Dulles, "John Paul II and the New Evangelization—What Does It Mean?" in *John Paul and the New Evangelization*, ed. Ralph Martin and Peter Williamson (San Francisco: Ignatius Press, 1995), 25.

1

peoples of Asia, Africa, the Americas, and India, particularly through its religious orders and congregations. There was little Protestant missionary effort until the nineteenth century.[2]

Second, without denying that Catholic missionary efforts have sometimes been accompanied by a cultural imperialism, coercion, and even violence, particularly in those days when the cross of the missionaries was accompanied by the sword of European conquerors and colonizers, there have also been significant efforts to discern the positive values in the cultures to be evangelized and to find a culturally appropriate expression for the Christian message. One thinks particularly of the Jesuits in India and China, but there are other examples.

Third, while Protestant evangelism is too often understood narrowly in terms of verbal proclamation, leading to a personal faith, the Catholic approach includes also proclaiming the good news of God's reign through word and example. Particularly in the contemporary Catholic Church, evangelization has a justice or liberation dimension.

Finally, the discovery in the sixteenth and seventeenth centuries of peoples living without knowledge of the gospel, as well as the encounter with the great religions of the world, has led to a rethinking in the Roman Catholic Church of the traditional doctrine, "no salvation outside the church." The Second Vatican Council acknowledged that God's saving grace can be effective in those who do not know Christ or his church (*Lumen gentium* 16) and that God's truth is often reflected in the great religions of the world (*Nostra aetate* 2). An implication of this development of doctrine is that evangelical efforts must remain always open to the mystery of God's presence in the other, whether religion or culture. A church aware of this mystery avoids the mistake of a one-sided

---

2. See Stephen Neill, *A History of Christian Missions* (Harmondsworth, England: Penguin Books, 1975), 210 ff.

proclamation; it is better equipped to enter into a genuine dialogue with others.

Evangelization since Vatican II

With the Second Vatican Council, the Catholic Church's understanding of its missionary task began to develop in a number of significant ways. First, the Council began a recovery of the word *evangelization* for Catholics. In contrast to Vatican I, which used the term *gospel* only once, Vatican II mentions the *gospel* 157 times, *evangelization* 31 times, and *evangelize* 18 times.[3] Shortly after the Council ended, Pope Paul VI changed the name of the Congregation for the Propagation of the Faith, established in 1622, to the Congregation for the Evangelization of Peoples, and he chose as the theme for the 1974 Synod of Bishops "the evangelization of the modern world."

Second, Pope Paul developed the concept of evangelization considerably. In *Evangelii nuntiandi* (1975), the great apostolic exhortation he issued after the 1974 Synod of Bishops on evangelization, he stressed that cultures, not just individuals, need to be evangelized.[4] And he emphasized that evangelization has a social dimension that involves human rights, family life, peace, justice, development, and liberation (no. 29). In the pope's view, evangelization and liberation are linked because the person "who is to be evangelized is not an abstract being but is subject to social and economic questions" (no. 31). Thus, there is a profound link in the pope's view between evangelization and social justice.

With Pope John Paul II evangelization moved to the center of the Catholic Church's understanding of its mission. Building on his

---

3. Dulles, "John Paul II and the New Evangelization," 26.
4. EN, *On Evangelization in the Modern World* (Washington, D.C.: United States Catholic Conference of Bishops, 1975).

predecessor's teaching, John Paul reaffirmed the place of works on behalf of justice in the church's evangelizing mission. He has also developed the understanding of evangelization in significant ways. While his 1991 encyclical *Redemptoris missio* emphasizes in no uncertain terms the importance of the traditional mission *ad gentes*, it also calls for a "new evangelization,"[5] a term he first used in his address to the Latin American bishops at their meeting at Port-au-Prince, Haiti, on March 9, 1983. Dulles lists the following four characteristics of the pope's *new* evangelization. First, it calls for the participation of every Christian, not just clerics and religious. Second, in being directed to those who have lost a living sense of their faith, it is distinct from the foreign missions. Third, it seeks to evangelize not just individuals, but cultures. Fourth, it envisages a comprehensive Christianization, a lifelong process of deepening the life of faith that includes catechetical teaching, moral doctrine, and the social teaching of the church, one that can lead ultimately to a "civilization of love."[6]

From the beginning of his pontificate John Paul II has shown a particular concern for the evangelization of culture. Shortly after his election, he established a special Pontifical Council for Culture and he continues to address cultural issues in his encyclicals. Yet, the effort to evangelize culture is a particular challenge.

Culture in a North American Context

Culture is a socially constructed environment, a world of symbolic forms, customs, and habits of the heart that embody meaning and value.[7] Cultures both shape us and are shaped by us. The term

---

5. *Redemptoris missio,* no. 30; *Origins* 20/34 (1991), 541–68.

6. Dulles, "John Paul II and the New Evangelization," 29–32.

7. For an excellent study, see Michael Paul Gallagher, *Clashing Symbols: An Introduction to Faith and Culture* (New York/Mahwah: Paulist Press, 1998).

culture is also used more generally to denote the values and lifestyle of a particular group or community within a larger society. Thus, it is difficult to speak merely of *culture*, for culture itself is diverse. As Pope John Paul suggests in *Redemptoris missio* (no. 37) with his image of the new Areopagus, our world today is rapidly changing. It is a world characterized by enormous movements of peoples, the juxtaposition of great wealth and great poverty, and the isolation and anonymity of the new "megalopolises." A new generation of young people is emerging, shaped not by their own traditions but by the mass media; at the same time, these media, compressing the boundaries of time and space, accelerate the process of modernization, creating a phenomenon that has been termed *globalization*.

Globalization brings about new problems. In a globalized world, not all cultures are equal. The influence of a rich and powerful culture like that of the United States contributes to common tastes in food, clothing, and entertainment, creating a type of "hyperculture." At the same time, the disruptive effect that this new mass culture, with its accompanying values, has on traditional cultures leads to what Robert Schreiter calls "particularization," a reassertion of identity that "include[s] newly (re)constructed cultures, so-called fundamentalisms, and the violent drawing of boundaries to try to keep out the modern world."[8] The terrorist attacks on the World Trade Center and the Pentagon on September 11, 2001, are a tragic symbol of this impulse.

In a North American context, culture presents its own challenges. The culture of the United States is at once individualistic, pluralistic, subjective, and as Dulles argues, consumerist. Robert Bellah attributes America's radical individualism to its Reformation heritage, to such an extent that he quotes G. K. Chesterton's famous remark that "in America, even the Catholics are

---

8. Robert J. Schreiter, "The World Church and Its Mission: A Theological Perspective," *Proceedings of the Canon Law Society of America* 59 (1997), 55.

Protestants."[9] Bellah sees this individualism as based on a sectarian Protestant emphasis on the right of individual conscience in matters of religious belief, without any corresponding sense for the common good. Calvin's doctrine of the divine transcendence as well as the Protestant emphasis on a near exclusive personal relationship with Jesus strengthened this radical individualism.[10]

Second, with its incredible blend of peoples, ethnicities, and religious traditions, American culture is diverse or pluralistic. The pictures of America in our national magazines after the September 11, 2001, terrorist attacks on New York and Washington showed Americans with white, black, and brown faces united in their common grief. We are a diverse people. And we are diverse religiously. According to Harvard University's "Pluralism Project" the United States has become the most religiously diverse country in the world.[11]

Third, American culture is profoundly subjective in its attitude toward truth. A profound skepticism about truth may well be its most basic characteristic. Religious arguments are not so much challenged as ignored. Since beliefs are private, all opinions are equally valid and none is really wrong. Religious diversity contributes to this privatizing of religious teachings. In platonic terms, the sophists have won. Truth is up to the individual; it has become exclusively personal. While in comparison to Europe a high level of Americans continue to identify themselves as Christians and pray daily, an increasing number, particularly among the elite, no longer practice their faith. Between 1991 and 1998, the proportion of those who stated no religious preference doubled, from 7 to 14 percent.

Many Christians, both from mainstream Protestant traditions as well as progressive Catholics, have been assimilated into this common

---

9. Robert N. Bellah, "Religion and the Shape of National Culture," *America* 181/3 (July 31–August 7, 1999), 10.

10. Ibid., 11–12.

11. Cf. Diane L. Eck, *A New Religious America: How a "Christian Country" Has Become the World's Most Religiously Diverse Nation* (HarperSanFrancisco, 2001).

culture. Their attitudes and values are largely shaped by its individual-istic, subjective, and anti-institutional spirit. Wade Clark Roof has emphasized the highly subjective approach to religion of the baby boomers, with their exaltation of experience and their fluid alliances.[12] Meredith McGuire writes about the "spiritual autonomy" of many contemporary believers who "feel free to choose components of their individual faith and practice, combining elements of their official reli-gious traditions with other culturally available elements."[13] More con-cretely, the attitudes of many Americans on questions such as premarital relations and cohabitation, marriage and divorce, homo-sexuality, and abortion are generally liberal. Their judgments reflect their secular culture, not biblical or church authority. On questions of personal morality, there is little difference between them and their completely secular neighbors, though liberal Christians are often much more open to issues of social justice. Many of those in their thir-ties and forties no longer practice their faith; they frequently consider themselves to be *spiritual* but not religious.

Conservative Christians, those associated with the "Christian right," whether in its Protestant or Catholic expression, claim to stand against mainstream American culture, though they are usually quite comfortable with the American free enterprise system, its for-eign policy, military actions, and the death penalty. Conservative Catholics decry a "culture of death," language of Pope John Paul II (now used also by President George W. Bush). Evangelical and fun-damentalist Protestants object to the dominance of "secular human-ism" in American culture. Though conservative Protestants have strong doctrinal differences with conservative Catholics, both groups have a great deal in common. Both have strong religious identities, giving them a clear sense of their "difference" from others. Both

---

12. Wade Clark Roof, *A Generation of Seekers: The Spiritual Journey of the Baby Boomer Generation* (San Francisco: HarperCollins, 1993), 8.

13. Meredith B. McGuire, "Mapping Contemporary American Spirituality: A Sociological Perspective," *Christian Spirituality Bulletin* 5/1 (1997), 4.

place great emphasis on authority, whether biblical or ecclesial. Both are easily supernaturalist in their worldviews, privileging faith positions over historical consciousness and scientific reason. But their inability to integrate modern modes of knowing with faith—in Catholic terms, to recognize the compatibility of faith and reason—means that the Christian right is not really able to enter into dialogue with a modern and postmodern culture. To this extent, its evangelical efforts will not be able to address the dominant culture. Its worldview is simply too different.

Thus, the culture the church seeks to evangelize in North America is very diverse. American Catholicism has been able to hold its Right, Center, and Left together in a single communion, but the stress lines are clearly evident, both among these groups and often with younger Catholics, particularly those who will be the church's future ministerial leaders. This, too, affects the Catholic Church's evangelical efforts, not the least because there is no common agreement on what evangelization means. We hope to address some of these issues in this book.

Cardinal Dulles's essay in Chapter 1 is both theoretical and personal; he probes the interdependence of culture and faith and reflects personally on how he was drawn to the Catholic faith by its embodiment in medieval and Renaissance culture. After reviewing the current "culture wars," he proposes some strategies for evangelization.

In Chapter 2 Laura Anzilotti surveys different approaches to evangelization in contemporary American Catholicism. She argues that the Catholic Right understands evangelization too narrowly, reducing it to making people Catholics; the Center tends to focus almost exclusively on the renewal of parochial life; and the Left risks identifying evangelization with church reform and social liberation.

Chapters 3 and 4 are centered on the parish. In Chapter 3 Robert S. Rivers draws on his considerable experience as a Paulist priest to discuss evangelization as a way of being church by placing it at the center of a parish's pastoral agenda. His particular concern is to move parishes from a "maintenance" mode to one of mission, one that embraces all parish programs and is concerned to change not just individuals but the world as well.

Chapter 4 explores the relation between evangelization and liturgy. Because many Catholics identify evangelization with preaching, going door to door, and inviting others into a personal relationship with Christ—in other words, as something "Protestant"—they are often unaware of the evangelical power of the liturgy. The final part considers three very different parishes that have been revitalized and transformed, with liturgy playing an important role.

In Chapter 5 Allan Figueroa Deck argues that U.S. Catholicism is seriously out of phase with worldwide Catholicism in terms of its reception of the Church's teaching on evangelization. He critiques a pastoral approach, that, preoccupied with inner church issues and doctrinal concerns, is not sufficiently open to social, cultural, and political contexts. He then identifies six issues critical to the evangelization of Hispanics in the United States.

Chapters 6 and 7 seek to help Catholics and Evangelicals deepen their understandings of evangelization by learning from each other. In Chapter 6, William Burrows gathers wisdom from both Catholic and Evangelical models of evangelization. His experience as a Catholic editor working with Evangelicals has enabled him to come to a greater appreciation of the Evangelical individualism so often criticized by Catholic commentators.

Chapter 7 is a contribution by Eddie Gibbs, an Evangelical scholar. He draws on his own experience as a missionary in Latin America and professor in an Evangelical seminary, as well as his study of popes Paul VI and John Paul II, to reflect on evangelization in the Catholic Church from an Evangelical perspective. At the end of his essay, he addresses some of the challenges raised by religious pluralism.

In Chapter 8 John Haughey, who has long been involved in Catholic/Evangelical dialogue, addresses the difficult question of proselytism. His essay seeks first to develop a theology of mission, particularly the place of the "great commission" (Matt 28:19) in such a theology, and then raises a number of ethical issues in relation to proselytism.

The final chapter by John Borelli shifts the discussion to the area of interreligious dialogue and mission. Borelli traces the idea that the church fulfills its evangelical mission through dialogue to the work of Pope Paul VI and to his desire for the church to engage the world with its religious diversity in conversation. In exploring the relationship between interreligious dialogue and mission, particularly in the teachings of Pope John Paul II, he also outlines some remaining tensions in official Catholicism, evident in the Congregation for the Doctrine of the Faith's Declaration, *Dominus Iesus* (November 5, 2000) and in its investigation of the work of Jesuit Father Jacques Dupuis.

Chapter 1

The Impact of the Catholic Church on American Culture

Avery Cardinal Dulles, S.J.

Two of the principal focuses of the pontificate of John Paul II
have been evangelization and the dialogue with culture. In the
vision of the pope, they are two aspects of a single mission. Paul VI
had already recognized this in his great apostolic exhortation,
Evangelii nuntiandi:

> The split between the Gospel and culture is without
> doubt the drama of our time, just as it was of other times.
> Therefore every effort must be made to ensure the full
> evangelization of culture, or more correctly of cultures.
> They have to be regenerated by an encounter with the
> Gospel. But this encounter will not take place if the
> Gospel is not proclaimed.[1]

The church is sent to transform the world in the light of the
gospel, but in order to do so it must take account of the soil in which

------

1. Paul VI, Apostolic Exhortation, *Evangelii nuntiandi* (1975), no. 20.

11

the gospel is to be planted. For this reason John Paul II stated in 1982: "Since the beginning of my pontificate I have considered the Church's dialogue with the cultures of our time to be a vital area, one in which the destiny of the world at the end of this twentieth century is at stake."[2]

The term *culture* is difficult to define. It is related to growth through human effort. We apply it (at least in English) to the raising of crops, flowers, and animals, as when we speak of agriculture, horti-culture, and oyster culture. But in common usage the term is now restricted to the human environment. Thus, John Paul II could declare, in a speech given to UNESCO in 1980: "Culture is a specific way of man's 'existing' and 'being.' Man always lives according to a culture which is specifically his, and which, in its turn, creates among men a tie which is also specifically theirs, determining the interhu-man and social character of human existence."[3] In a speech at Coimbra, Portugal, in 1982, he set forth three theses: culture is *of* man; culture is *from* man, and culture is *for* man. It is *of* man because it is proper to human beings to have cultures. Brute animals are at most passive recipients of the effects of human culture; they have no culture of their own. Culture is *from* man, because human beings freely construct it according to their own decisions and creative pow-ers. Culture, finally, is *for* man, because human beings are the prin-cipal beneficiaries of culture. By means of it they perfect themselves.[4]

Culture should also be seen as a social rather than a merely indi-vidual reality. It affects people in groups. But not everything collective

---

2. John Paul II, Letter to Cardinal Agostino Casaroli instituting the Pontifical Council for Culture, May 20, 1982; text in *L'Osservatore Romano* (English weekly edition), June 28, 1982, 19–20, at 19.

3. John Paul II, "Address to the United Nations Educational, Scientific and Cultural Organization," Paris, June 2, 1980, no. 6; text in Joseph Gremillion, ed., *The Church and Culture Since Vatican II* (Notre Dame, Ind.: University of Notre Dame Press, 1985), 187–97, at 189.

4. John Paul II, "Address to Intellectuals and Scientists," Coimbra, Portugal, no. 3; text in *Origins* 12 (May 27, 1982), 27–29, at 27.

is a matter of culture. The cultural order has to do with the customs and values that people freely embrace, and for this reason it can be distinguished from the political and economic orders, in which the reigning system is more impersonal and coercive. A culture, rather than being externally imposed, is interiorized in the community that accepts it. For that very reason, it is less tangible and more elusive than organized forms of society.

It may also be said that culture pertains above all to the human spirit, and to the body only in relation to the spirit. Food insofar as it nourishes the body is a matter of chemistry or biology, but insofar as meals are an occasion for conversation and social life, they are cultural events.

Although it would be too ambitious to give a general definition of culture, I may say that for present purposes the term can be taken to mean the sum of the ways in which a people nurtures, expresses, and sustains the inner life of its members. I understand it to be a system of meanings, historically transmitted, embodied in customs and symbols, and instilled into new members of the group, so that they are inclined to think, judge, and act in characteristic ways.[5]

The culture of a people manifests itself on many different planes. It includes their styles of speech and mutual intercourse, including their meals, dress, dwellings, and patterns of social behavior. It exists on the level of popular customs, in the ways that people celebrate birth, puberty, marriage, and death. It is found also at the level of "high culture," that is to say, in philosophy, literature, painting, sculpture, architecture, music, and the other arts. In the common estimation, a person of culture is one who is distinguished for refinement of taste and manners.

For present purposes, I shall use the term *culture* in a broadly sociological sense. Wherever human society exists, culture is present.

---

5. This is approximately the definition I proposed in *The Reshaping of Catholicism* (San Francisco: Harper & Row, 1988), 40.

According to the influence it has on its participants, a culture can be good, bad, or indifferent. But an evil culture, one that dehumanizes people, can also be called an anticulture. In an address of 1984, John Paul II speaks of an "anticulture which reveals itself, among other ways, in growing violence, murderous confrontations, exploitation of instincts and selfish interests."[6] In *Evangelium vitae* and elsewhere, the pope describes the clash between what he calls the cultures of life and of death.

Culture and religion are intimately connected. Christopher Dawson points out: "Every great civilization that exists in the world today has a great religious tradition associated with it, and it is impossible to understand the culture unless we understand the religion that lies behind it."[7] John Paul II puts the matter very succinctly: "At the heart of every culture lies the attitude man takes to the greatest mystery: the mystery of God. Different cultures are basically different ways of facing the question of the meaning of personal existence. When this question is eliminated, the culture and moral life of nations are corrupted."[8]

Christianity as a revealed religion has a very complex relationship to culture.[9] It came to birth in the highly developed culture of Palestine, at a point where Jewish, Greek, and Roman cultures intersected. It drew its vocabulary, images, rituals, and organization in great part from the Judaism of the day. It then matured as a religion

6. John Paul II, "Address to the Second Annual Meeting of the Pontifical Council for Culture," January 16, 1984; in Gremillion, *Church and Culture*, 207–9, at 209.

7. Christopher Dawson, "The Institutional Forms of Christian Culture," in *Christianity and European Culture: Selections from the Work of Christopher Dawson*, ed. Gerald J. Russello (Washington, D.C.: Catholic University of America Press, 1998), 54–64, at 56.

8. John Paul II, Encyclical, *Centesimus annus* (1991), no. 24.

9. For a schematization of the ways in which Christians have seen the relations between the gospel and culture, one may still profitably consult the classic work of H. Richard Niebuhr, *Christ and Culture* (New York: Harper & Row, 1951).

by interacting with other cultures of the ancient world—notably those of Greece and Rome. Christianity therefore never has existed, and could not conceivably exist, without culture. Human cultures have always provided it with the languages and visible forms by which it expresses and communicates itself. For this reason, we may say that in some sense Christianity depends on culture.[10] Conversely, however, faith makes an impact on culture. The culture of Judaism was profoundly marked by the faith of ancient Israel. Christian revelation further modified and transformed that culture, producing its own style of speech, behavior, and worship. The relationship between faith and culture is therefore a dialectical one of mutual interdependence.

Precisely at this point a problem arises. If the relationship is mutual, it would seem that just as cultures can be transformed by Christianity, so Christianity can be transformed by cultures. It can in fact be denatured, so that it ceases to be itself, as is the case when syncretism occurs. Protestant liberal theologians of the late nineteenth century generally took the position that Christianity had been corrupted by Hellenization in the early centuries. But the Catholic Church, like the Orthodox, considers that the encounter with Hellenistic civilization was a providential occurrence that helped Christian faith and social existence to attain maturity.

Although it immerses itself in cultures and interacts with them, Christianity is never reducible to a given culture or any combination of cultures. As a divine revelation it stands above all cultures, challenging and criticizing them. Because every culture is finite and deficient, no one cultural embodiment can reflect the full power of the word of God. Christianity, therefore, is most fittingly expressed in a

---

10. Joseph Ratzinger put the matter well in Hong Kong in March 1993: "Faith itself is culture. There is no such thing as naked faith or mere religion. Simply stated, insofar as faith tells man who he is and how he should begin being human, faith creates culture." See Joseph Cardinal Ratzinger, "Christ, Faith, and the Challenge of Cultures," *Origins* 24 (March 30, 1995), 679–86, at 682.

variety of cultures. According to Vatican II's Constitution on the Church, the church "fosters and takes to herself, insofar as they are good, the ability, resources, and customs of each people. Taking them to herself, she purifies, strengthens, and ennobles them" (*Lumen gentium* 13). As this quotation indicates, the church has, or should have, a threefold relationship to culture. It selects what is true and good; it purifies what it selects, separating it from the dross that is unworthy of the gospel. Third, the church elevates even the finest fruits of human endeavor by turning them into instruments for the transmission of the truth and grace that come from God.

Although every culture may have something positive to offer, we cannot assume that all are equally well-suited to be bearers of the gospel. An inferior and debased culture can only distort or reject the truth of God's word. But a culture that is humanly good and sound can show forth, to some limited extent, the truth, beauty, and goodness of the Christian faith.

A culture that is naturally healthy is surely the best vehicle for the gospel, especially if that culture has been subjected to a prolonged and intimate contact with Christian faith. A culture that has matured under the influence of the gospel may be called a Christian culture. It serves as a relatively fitting instrument for communicating the superlative riches of Christ and his message of salvation.

As a revealed religion, Christianity is in some way supracultural. It can never be exhaustively incorporated into any given culture. All cultures fall short. Even while using them, the human spirit, reaching out to the divine, senses their limitations. Christianity, therefore, includes an apophatic dimension. As its own asymptotic limit, Christianity aspires to a humanly impossible condition in which it dispenses with words and images, confronting the divine reality in naked purity. This was the grain of truth at the heart of the iconoclastic heresy. In the conditions of this present life, faith and culture exist in a kind of mutual interdependence. Culture stands to benefit from faith, which helps it to discern what is rich and noble in any given human system and to correct what is deficient. Faith, conversely, benefits from culture, because it uses the resources of various cultures to probe the meaning of revelation and give it better liturgical and intellectual expression. "A faith that does not become culture," says John Paul II, "is a faith that has not been fully received, not fully and thoroughly thought through, not fully lived out."[11]

Some Personal Reflections

To give concrete form to the principles I have been stating in abstract language, I should like to make some autobiographical remarks. In my own approach to Christian faith, I was greatly assisted by my exposure as a boy to the cultures of the high Middle Ages and the Renaissance. The process began with a spring vacation that I spent in Italy in 1932. Like other tourists, I visited innumerable cathedrals and museums, and was impressed by the inner coherence between the religious themes and the aesthetic quality of the masterpieces I admired. In my adolescent years, I continued to feel the attraction of the art and literature of this Christian past. Later on, as a college student at Harvard, I delved more deeply into medieval and Renaissance culture, including the philosophy and theology of those centuries. Bernard of Clairvaux, Thomas Aquinas, Dante, Fra Angelico, Chaucer, and the cathedral of Chartres provided clear evidence that Catholic Christianity, when deeply held in the hearts of a people, was capable of generating an intellectual and artistic culture of the highest caliber. I also developed a taste for the art and literature of the Catholic Reformation in Italy, Spain, and France.

Gradually, through further study, I came to discover that the culture-forming capacity of Catholic Christianity was not exhausted by the past. In contemporary France, I noted, philosophers such as Etienne Gilson and Jacques Maritain, artists such as Georges

---

11. John Paul II, Letter to Casaroli, 19.

Rouault, and poets such as Charles Péguy and Paul Claudel could still flourish. Many of the finest English-speaking authors, including T. S. Eliot, James Joyce, and Ezra Pound, were living off the capital of a Catholic heritage that gave power and elegance to their work even though they were not, or did not remain, Roman Catholics. The culture of Western Europe and America in our days seemed to me like an empty bottle, still emitting the sweet scent of a perfume it had once held. But the fragrance was diminishing, since the faith from which it arose was in recession.

A further fact that entered into my process of conversion was the existence of popular Catholicism, as I witnessed it in a city such as Cambridge, Massachusetts. The Catholic faith had an extraordinary hold on the minds and hearts of the common people, most of whom, in that region, were of Irish extraction. They were remarkably faithful in their religious observance. Their piety was governed by the same revelation that had inspired the great artists and poets of earlier centuries.

A critical moment in my approach to Roman Catholicism took place when I entered a Catholic church one Sunday evening and found it full of working-class men and women singing Latin hymns that I was able to recognize as the work of Thomas Aquinas. Only later did I find out that I was attending the Benediction of the Blessed Sacrament, at which the O *Salutaris hostia* and the *Tantum ergo* were regularly sung. The culture handed down from medieval Europe was still a living reality in the Catholic Church.

About the time that I came into the church, in 1940, I became aware of Catholicism in the United States as a multicultural reality. In different parts of the country it was kept alive by immigrant groups from Western Europe that settled in ethnic ghettos—French, German, Italian, Irish, and Polish. Although the dominant culture of the nation was secular, and had only a veneer of Christianity, there was a variety of authentically Catholic subcultures scattered throughout the United States. They had little impact on the nation as a whole, but they maintained themselves with remarkable power. These subcultures, as I perceived them, were not divisive. Reflecting different ways of assimilating the one apostolic faith, they were held in unity by Catholic dogma, ritual, and hierarchical authority.

About the time of World War II, Catholicism in the United States burst out of its various ghettos and flowed into the mainstream of American life. Individuals and nuclear families migrated to any part of the country where the demands of military service or civil employment dictated. Mixed marriages became common. The more affluent Catholics moved from the inner cities to the suburbs.

For a while it appeared that Catholicism might become a Christianizing cultural force similar to that which Protestantism had been in the previous century. Catholics advanced to top positions in business and the professions. The election of John F. Kennedy as the first Catholic president seemed to have great symbolic significance. Bishop Fulton J. Sheen became a television idol. Catholic publishers and universities enjoyed unprecedented success and prestige.

But Catholicism had scarcely started to bloom when the blight set in. The hope that Catholics, by entering into the mainstream, would be able to set the tone for the broader culture proved illusory. American Catholics, having been up to now in a culturally inferior position, cast envious eyes upon their Protestant and Jewish colleagues and strove to emulate them. They lost confidence in their own religious and cultural heritage and sought to become more typically American in their attitudes. Many Catholics diluted their faith or became schizophrenic—Catholic by religion and secular by culture. A chasm began to open up between the faith and culture of American Catholics.

As recent popes have reminded us, the split between faith and culture is an unhealthy thing for both. Faith cannot achieve its full effect unless it finds symbols and other cultural vehicles whereby it can be transmitted and cherished in the minds and hearts of believers. A faith that fails to find fitting cultural expressions becomes anemic.

Culture, on the other hand, suffers by lack of exposure to the gospel. In the absence of strong religious influences, it falls under the domination of the natural human desires for riches, comforts, and security.

Since the 1970s the United States has been racked by what various authors have described as "culture wars." On the one side are conservatives who hold that there are transcendently grounded and enduring moral laws, and on the other side are progressives who wish to revise all concepts of truth and falsehood, right and wrong in light of the prevailing assumptions of contemporary life.[12] The legitimacy of practices such as abortion, euthanasia, homosexual relations, divorce, and contraception has been bitterly controverted in the nation at large. Orthodox Jews, Evangelical Protestants, and practicing Catholics tend to stand together against a growing coalition of liberal Jews, liberal Protestants, and secular humanists. This second group seeks to liberate society from the Judeo-Christian hegemony and to establish a "cultural pluralism" in which all religions and ideologies are treated as equal.

The dominant culture of the United States today is frequently, and, I think correctly, called consumerist. Driven by the laws of the market, it treats everything, including religion, as a marketable product. So powerful is this secular culture, conveyed through the mass media of communication, that it brooks almost no resistance from religious or other factions. Although religion is very much a part of the national scene in the United States, it has only slight influence on the dominant culture. The popular media treat religion as an option for people who happen to feel religious, but not as a truth that demands acceptance. Typical newspapers relegate stories about religion to the Style Section, unless they can shock their readers with reports of scandalous misconduct, in which case the stories receive greater prominence.

---

12. James Davison Hunter, *Culture Wars: The Struggle to Define America* (New York: Basic Books, 1991), 44–45.

Consumerism breeds subjectivism and supports hedonism. Describing the consumerist culture, Pope John Paul II writes in *Centesimus annus*: "People are ensnared in a web of false and superficial gratifications rather than helped to experience their personhood in an authentic way" (CA 41). If one surveys films, television programs, the statistics on marriage, divorce, abortions, births out of wedlock, and the like, it appears that the vast majority of Americans are driven by the search for wealth, comforts, and pleasures rather than by loyalty to Christian doctrinal and moral principles. In view of original sin, this problem is constant and perennial, but it seems to have become more acute in the past half century. It is too early to judge whether the present encounter with terrorism will produce a lasting change.

The popes have repeatedly called for a greater engagement between faith and culture. The dialogue must be conducted with the realization that, as the present pope reminds us, the faith "does not spring spontaneously from any cultural soil."[13] Faith comes through divine revelation, passed down in history. If it becomes imbedded in a culture, care must be taken to prevent the culture from dictating its own terms. Faith therefore has to be implanted in the culture by a process that John Paul II describes as "apostolic dialogue."[14] Only when solidly rooted in the apostolic tradition can faith bring about an authentic evangelization of cultures.

Evangelization Strategies for U.S. Catholics

The problem in the United States and, I suspect, in most of Western Europe as well, is to find ingredients in the reigning culture that can serve as vehicles of faith, as the Fathers were able to draw elements from the Greco-Roman culture they inherited. American Catholics have been asking themselves whether they can find a point

13. John Paul II, Apostolic Exhortation, *Catechesi tradendae* (1979), §53.
14. Ibid.

of insertion for Catholicism in the American tradition or whether Catholic culture must be introduced into that tradition from outside.

In the 1950s, a leading American Catholic intellectual, Father John Courtney Murray, took a bold initiative. He sought to move the Catholic Church from the margins to the center of American life by proposing a Catholic interpretation of the Declaration of Independence and other founding documents of our national life. Although he was aware of the nominalist and utilitarian currents in the thought of writers like Thomas Jefferson, and Jefferson's mentor John Locke, he considered it possible to find a realist metaphysics implicit in the claim of the Declaration of Independence that all men had been endowed by their Creator with certain inalienable rights, including life, liberty, and the pursuit of happiness. The American philosophy of natural rights could in this way be anchored in the venerable traditions of natural law and natural theology. On this hypothesis, Catholics could eagerly participate in the American consensus, and the nation could perhaps be saved from the relativism and pragmatism by which it seemed even then to be threatened. Anxious to avoid any control of the church by the state, Murray was willing to accept the American system of separation of church and state and to rely on voluntary participation, rather than governmental help, for the support of the churches.

Murray's brilliant strategy, based on careful study of the materials, continues to this day to attract disciples, especially intellectuals identified with the *neoconservative* movement. But, as Murray was aware before he died in 1967, the efficacy of his strategy depended on persuading non-Catholic Americans to share his reading of the founding documents. Since his death, the leading political philosophers and jurists have drifted far away from realist metaphysics in the direction of agnosticism and subjectivism.

On the pretext that religion is an essentially private matter, to be settled in the sanctuary of the individual conscience, the courts have progressively exiled churches and other religious institutions from the public arena. The tone of American public life, as reflected in government-supported schools and universities and in the public media of information and entertainment, has become increasingly secular. Churches survive, and in some cases are relatively well attended, but they are marginal to the ethos of the nation.

Within the Catholic Church itself, a number of voices accuse Murray and his disciples of having betrayed authentic Catholic culture and sold out to liberalism. Traditionalists maintain that Catholics should forge a culture based on their own integral heritage. In so doing, many of them turn to Western European models. With a certain nostalgia for a time when the church was culturally dominant, they celebrate the theology of *ressourcement*, which flourished in France after World War II. Unwilling to compromise with the secular culture of the day, they seem satisfied to create small oases where they can cultivate the riches of Catholic tradition and criticize the larger society. In this way, one might think, they can preserve the best of the past, as did the monks in the age of the barbarian invasions of Europe. Perhaps they can also plant the seeds of a future Catholic culture that will be at home in our nation.

Besides the strategies of neoconservatism and *ressourcement* of which I have just been speaking, there is a third option: to build on the popular religion of immigrant ethnic groups that actually practice the faith in their own American neighborhoods. This process worked reasonably well before World War II, when the clan and the neighborhood did so much to transmit Catholic sensibilities in new generations. Most of these ethnic enclaves, as I have mentioned, are much weaker today. But the waves of recent immigration from the Philippines, Vietnam, Korea, and Latin America have produced new centers of Catholic culture. In particular, the large and growing Hispanic presence arouses great hope and interest.

Contemporary American Catholicism is being deeply affected by the influx of immigrants from Cuba, Puerto Rico, the Dominican Republic, Mexico, and other Spanish-speaking countries of Central and South America. In some parts of the country, especially the Southwest, the Catholic presence today is predominantly Hispanic. These Latinos, although many of them have become lax in their sacramental practice, remain culturally Catholic. They inherit popular devotions and customs passed down for generations in their communities. To the extent that they retain or recover their Catholic identity, they may be able to provide a Catholic communal presence that offsets the individualism and agnosticism of the broader culture.[15]

The prognosis is uncertain. There is a serious danger that this Hispanic American population, intent upon success in American terms, will forget or repudiate its own roots and adopt the prevailing American values of individualism, professionalism, and worldly success. Alarming numbers of Latinos have been embracing Evangelical Protestantism or Pentecostalism. And even if the Hispanic American population were to become fully committed to Catholicism, their forms of piety would probably prove unsuitable to most other Americans. Thus, the problem of evangelizing American culture would still remain.

Conclusion

On a visit to Los Angeles in 1987, Pope John Paul II was informed by Archbishop Rembert Weakland that the United States has the largest number of educated Catholics in the world. After expressing satisfaction with this information, the pope responded that in that case the church should be in a position to exercise a strong influence upon American culture. Then he put forth the questions:

---

15. On this subject, see Orlando O. Espín, "Popular Catholicism among Latinos," in Jay P. Dolan and Allan Figueroa Deck, eds., *Hispanic Catholic Culture in the U.S.: Issues and Concerns* (Notre Dame, Ind.: University of Notre Dame Press, 1994), 308–59.

But how is the American culture evolving today? Is this evolution being influenced by the Gospel? Does it clearly reflect Christian inspiration? Your music, your poetry, your art, your drama, your painting and sculpture, the literature you are producing—are all these things which reflect the soul of a nation being influenced by the spirit of Christ for the perfection of humanity?[16]

In issuing this challenge, the Holy Father was calling attention to the connection between faith and the higher manifestations of culture in the artistic sphere, which have traditionally served as instruments of evangelization. His questions, I suspect, were rhetorical, since he knew that they would have to be answered in the negative.

Archbishop Weakland himself, ten years later, confirmed the pope's judgment. He devoted an important lecture to the thesis that Catholics in America have produced very little in the arts that can be seen as expressing who they are and what they believe. The culture of the Catholic people, he said, is indistinguishable from that of America in general. Because Americans have not given suitable form to their beliefs, they are seriously hampered in transmitting the faith to the next generation.[17]

I do not wish to exaggerate. A handful of excellent Catholic novelists, poets, painters, and sculptors could certainly be named. But many of the most prominent Catholic intellectuals have turned against their roots and embraced the contemporary secular culture. They urge the pope and the bishops to abandon traditional Catholic moral and doctrinal standards, accommodating the church to the

16. John Paul II, "Response to Archbishop Rembert Weakland," Los Angeles, September 16, 1987; *Origins* 17 (October 1, 1987), 263.

17. Archbishop Rembert G. Weakland, "Aesthetic and Religious Experience in Evangelization," *Theology Digest* 44 (Winter, 1997), 319–29.

times. Some reach for notoriety by demeaning and ridiculing the sacred symbols of their former spiritual home.

For the most part, Catholic universities, which should be matrices of Catholic culture, have been of little assistance. Although they serve to maintain some links between the academy and the church, they are driven by the forces of the market to attract and form students for attaining success in an economically competitive society. While in most respects imitating their secular counterparts, they struggle to transmit a modicum of the Catholic tradition in theology, philosophy, literature, and art.

To end on a more practical and positive note, I suggest that there are loci in the ordinary life of the church where faith is to some degree "becoming culture." The Catholic Church in the United States is a strong religious institution with more than sixty million members, nearly a quarter of the total population. It is efficiently organized under a body of bishops who are for the most part loyal to Rome, energetic, and pastorally prudent. It has significant cultural assets inherited from the nations from which its members originally came.

In the parishes, there is a growing sense of the need to build up communities whose values, grounded in the gospel, provide a clear alternative to the dominant culture. Parents are striving to discern the culture that shapes the imagination of the young and to provide a healthy moral and religious environment for their children. Many well-to-do Catholics are regularly putting themselves in touch with the poor and the marginalized. Local parishes and retreat centers are finding ways of retrieving the spiritual traditions of Catholicism and translating them for lay people living in our complex world. The popularity of various new movements such as the Catholic Worker, the Focolare, Communion and Liberation, and the charismatic renewal, especially among the young, is a hopeful sign.

It is too early to judge what effects the recent acts of terrorism may have on our American culture. The mood has certainly changed, but a mood does not constitute a culture. It seems possible, however, that current events will shake us out of our individualism, hedonism, and consumerism. The nation is feeling the need for guideposts that can bear up in seasons of failure and anxiety. At least in the New York area, where I live, the Catholic Church has been a strong presence, enabling people to ritualize their grief and refocus their hopes in such a way as to taste, even here on Earth, the fruits of Christ's redemptive work. In its hour of peril, our nation would seem to be more open to the church's message of truth and love than ever before.

In a sense, we may speak of a "Catholic moment"—a moment of opportunity if we can make it so. The Catholic Church is uniquely positioned to set the problems of the day in a moral and religious framework so that they can be addressed with serenity and confidence. As the church engages in a patient but insistent dialogue with culture, it will gain strength for the performance of its primary mission, which is to transform the lives of all men and women by bringing them into communion with Jesus Christ, and in this sense to evangelize.

Chapter 2

Evangelization: Three Contemporary Approaches

Laura Niemann Anzilotti

Christians of all denominations cite: "Go, therefore, and make disciples of all nations, baptizing them in the name of the Father, and of the Son and of the holy Spirit" (Matt 28:19) as Christ's missionary mandate to his followers. From this one passage stems a myriad of Evangelical activities: from revival tent preaching to contemplative prayer for the conversion of non-Christians. The dichotomy in Evangelical activity exists not only within Christianity as a whole, but also within Catholicism. This chapter explores the Catholic Church's postconciliar teaching on its evangelical mission and compares it to various approaches to evangelization in the United States representing the Catholic Right, Center, and Left, to answer the questions: Are we evangelizing as one unified church? And if not, how should these approaches be adjusted so that all participate fully in the "new evangelization"?

Evangelization Since Vatican II

In order to answer these questions, one must examine recent church teaching on evangelization. As Timothy McCarthy notes, prior to Vatican II, the church used a dualistic language to express its mission. Evangelization and conversion comprised the primary, supernatural mission of the church while works of mercy and charity were seen as its secondary, natural mission.[1] Though Vatican II was less dualistic in its theology, its description of the church's mission still implied a dualism of religious and secular ends. The Council Fathers maintained that "Christ…gave his Church no proper mission in the political, economic or social order. The purpose which he set before her is a religious one" (*Gaudium et Spes* 42). The Council asserted that one fulfills Christ's religious mandate through missionary activity: "The specific purpose of this missionary activity is evangelization and the planting of the Church among those peoples and groups where she has not yet taken root" (*Ad gentes* 6). While the Council equated mission with evangelization, it did not specifically link it to action on behalf of those suffering injustice.

But in the postconciliar period, a more unified vision of the church's mission began to emerge. The Episcopal Synod of 1971, like the Council, equated the church's mission with evangelization. However, unlike the Council, the Synod linked evangelization to liberation, asserting that "the mission of proclaiming the gospel in our times requires that we commit ourselves to man's integral liberation, here and now, in our earthly existence."[2] In an oft-repeated statement, the Synod document stated: "Action on behalf of justice and participation in the transformation of the world fully appear to us as a constitutive dimension of the preaching of the Gospel, or, in other words, of the Church's mission for the redemption of the human race and its liberation from every oppressive situation" (no. 6).

---

1. Timothy G. McCarthy, *The Catholic Tradition: Before and After Vatican II: 1878–1993* (Chicago: Loyola Press, 1998), 76–77.

2. "Justice in the World," in Michael Walsh and Brian Davies, eds., *Proclaiming Justice and Peace: Documents from John XXIII to John Paul II* (Mystic, Conn.: Twenty-third Publications, 1985), no. 35.

Pope Paul VI continued to join mission, evangelization, and liberation in his 1975 apostolic exhortation, *Evangelii nuntiandi,* when he questioned: "How in fact can one proclaim the new Commandment without promoting in justice and in peace the true, authentic advancement of man?"[3] Thus the Synod of 1971 and Pope Paul VI inextricably linked mission, evangelization, and the advancement of humanity.

Pope John Paul II and the "New Evangelization"

Pope John Paul II also linked mission, evangelization, and liberation and placed them at the heart of the church's mission.[4] In his 1991 encyclical *Redemptoris missio (RM)* and his 1999 apostolic letter *Ecclesia in America (EA)* he outlined a "new evangelization."[5] Theologians offer several hypotheses as to what makes this evangelization "new." Avery Dulles claims that the pope links the new evangelization to a reevangelization of formerly Christian areas.[6] Timothy McCarthy states that "the new evangelization involves a participation in the threefold mission of Jesus who taught, witnessed and served."[7] Dave Nodar writes that several elements distinguish new evangelization. It is Christocentric, a responsibility of the entire people of God, emphasizes local not foreign missionary work, evangelizes entire cultures, and includes a missionary spirituality.[8]

---

3. Pope Paul VI, *Evangelii nuntiandi,* in Michael Walsh and Brian Davies, eds., *Proclaiming Justice and Peace: Documents from John XXIII to John Paul II* (Mystic, Conn.: Twenty-third Publications, 1985), no. 31.

4. Thomas P. Rausch, *Reconciling Faith and Reason: Apologists, Evangelists, and Theologians in a Divided Church* (Collegeville, Minn.: Liturgical Press, 2000), 101.

5. John Paul II, *Redemptoris missio,* Origins 20/34 (1991), 541–68; *Ecclesia in America,* Origins 28 (1999), 566–92.

6. Avery Dulles, "John Paul and the New Evangelization," *America* 166 (Feb. 1, 1992), 57.

7. McCarthy, *The Catholic Tradition,* 80.

8. Dave Nodar, "What Are the Characteristics of the New Evangelization?" http://www.christlife.org/evangelization/articles/C_newevan.html, 2000.

Recognizing that many interpretations of the new evangelization exist, Cardinal Roger M. Mahony suggested at the consistory of May 21–24, 2001, the preparation of a "Directory on the New Evangelization," saying the term "new evangelization" has been much used and now needs to be better defined.[9]

Despite the varied interpretations of the new evangelization, John Paul II clearly builds on Paul VI's concept of evangelization while adding new emphases. All Catholics, not just the clergy and religious, should proclaim the gospel. "No believer in Christ, no institution of the Church can avoid this supreme duty: to proclaim Christ to all peoples" (RM 3). Yet one does not evangelize in isolation from the church. "Mission is seen as a community commitment, a responsibility of the local church" (RM 27). Therefore, the bishops, as shepherds of the particular churches, are ultimately responsible for evangelizing efforts (RM 63).

Within the context of the episcopally led community, Christians must deepen their personal relationship with Jesus Christ so that they may evangelize effectively (EA 68). "Through their own spiritual experiences…there will emerge an ever increasing dedication to the new evangelization in America" (EA 7). One deepens her relationship with the Lord by encountering him in the scriptures, the liturgy, the poor (EA 12), and in prayer (EA 29). This encounter with Jesus is essential because "we cannot preach conversion unless we ourselves are converted anew everyday" (RM 47).

After Christians renew their relationship with Christ, whom do they evangelize? The answer presents a distinctive element of the new evangelization. It focuses on evangelization "in countries with ancient Christian roots, and occasionally in the younger Churches as well, where entire groups of the baptized have lost a living sense of faith" (RM 33). Thus, the new evangelization, in part, requires people's reevangelization. New evangelization also continues more

---

9. "Consistory of Cardinals Meets with Pope," America 184 (June 4–11, 2001), 4–5.

traditional evangelization of people who have not accepted Christ or his church. In this evangelization, ecumenical and interreligious dialogue are essential "as a method and means of mutual knowledge and enrichment" (*RM* 55). Dialogue should not be tactical evangelization, but a means of enriching each side and removing mutual prejudice (*RM* 56).

Another group to evangelize is the poor. In fact, John Paul II's "preferential love for the poor" means that they should be the first recipients of evangelization, one that encompasses social justice (*EA* 54). Nevertheless, he warns readers that "it is not the Church's mission to work directly on the economic, technical or political levels….Rather her mission consists essentially in offering people an opportunity not to 'have more' but to 'be more'" (*RM* 58). Through these words, John Paul reminds the church that the poor must be the first to hear the gospel and that the aim of evangelization must remain Jesus Christ, not material advancement.

Yet John Paul II stresses not only the conversion of the individual but the "clearly conceived, serious and well-organized effort to evangelize the culture" (*EA* 70). In this genuinely new element of evangelization, Christians will inculturate the gospel, he claims, through education (*EA* 71), the media (*EA* 72), a commitment to peace, justice, and liberation, and safeguarding the created world (*RM* 37). Proclaiming Jesus Christ and inculturating the gospel

> constitutes the Church's first and fundamental way of serving the coming of the kingdom in individuals and in human society….The Church then serves the kingdom by establishing communities….But it must be immediately added that this temporal dimension of the kingdom remains incomplete unless it is related to the kingdom of Christ present in the Church. (*RM* 20)

Thus, John Paul II asserts that evangelization's purpose is to bring individuals and societies to Christ, with community and the church as necessary ways of encountering him.

Different Approaches to Evangelization

The late Cardinal Bernardin recognized that a serious polarization exists among conservative, centrist, and liberal Catholics. He lamented that "ideas, journals and leaders are pressed to align themselves with pre-existing camps and are viewed warily when they depart from those expectations."[10] Unfortunately, the "fear and polarization" that Bernardin noted currently extends into the area of evangelization. Catholics on the Right, in the Center, or on the Left do not always share the same evangelical vision articulated by Pope John Paul II as bringing people to Christ through community and church.

The Catholic Right is represented by the "new apologists" who seem to be the most concerned with evangelization. In their books, magazines, and tapes, apologists like Karl Keating, Peter Kreeft, Scott Hahn, and Patrick Madrid stress complete adherence to the church's teachings, whether dogmatic or doctrinal. Well-coordinated Internet sites effectively disseminate their thoughts. The *New Oxford Review* and *National Catholic Register* as well as the English translation of *L'Osservatore Romano* also reflect the Right while Thomas Aquinas College in California and Franciscan University of Steubenville (Ohio) serve as meccas for an apologetic approach to Catholic faith and evangelization.

The Catholic Center is represented by the National Conference of Catholic Bishops (NCCB) and the United States Catholic Conference (USCC), two distinct but closely related organizations. The NCCB's membership consists of all the Catholic

---

10. Cardinal Joseph Bernardin, "Called to Be Catholic: Church in a Time of Peril," *Origins* 26/11 (1996), 167.

bishops in the United States who represent every spectrum of the Catholic Right, Center, and Left while the USCC committees include lay, clergy, and religious who recommend policy to the body of bishops. The organizations' documents and decisions reflect discussions and compromises among contrasting perspectives, both clerical and lay, and the organizations themselves become centrist. For example, when the NCCB issued "Faithful Citizenship," a pamphlet about American Catholics' duty to vote in the 2000 election, the Catholic Right protested that the bishops did not demand that Catholics vote for pro-life candidates. Similarly, the Catholic Left complained that the bishops neglected to equate Catholic social teaching with voting for a candidate.[11] The NCCB–USCC, reorganized on July 1, 2001, as the United States Conference of Catholic Bishops (USCCB), sits squarely in the American Catholic Center.

The USCCB disseminates teachings and letters through the weekly documentary service *Origins* as well as through its Internet site. Most important, the conference's ideas are spread through the liturgical and parish life that the bishops oversee. The Secretariat for Evangelization and its plethora of conferences and activities shows the USCCB's dedication to evangelization.

The Catholic Left is represented by much of the theological academy as well as by organizations such as Call to Action, Corpus, Dignity, We Are Church, the Women's Ordination Conference, and the National Coalition of American Nuns, all advocating the importance of reform within the church. Progressive or liberal publications such as *America, Commonweal,* and the *National Catholic Reporter* often feature articles from prominent Catholic reformers, who are frequently associated with liberal theology departments such as the University of Notre Dame and Boston College.

The thrust of reformist Catholics certainly differs from the doctrinal emphasis of the Catholic Right and the parochial thrust of the

---

11. Paul Baumann, "Counting Votes," *Commonweal* 127 (November 3, 2000), 7–8.

Catholic Center. Similarly, these different groups do not coalesce in the definition, methods, and goals of evangelization. Yet, do any of the three coalesce with the aims of John Paul II's new evangelization?

The Catholic Right

For many on the Right, evangelization is identical with bringing people into the Catholic Church. Karl Keating, a popular apologist in the United States, runs *Catholic Answers*, a lay organization of apologetics and evangelization. Keating defines evangelization as

> spreading the Good News of Jesus Christ as it has been entrusted to the Church he established. When we evangelize we explain the truths of the Catholic faith and invite people to consider them and consider becoming Catholics.[12]

Just as Keating equates evangelization with explaining the Catholic faith, so, too, does *Envoy Magazine*, edited by Patrick Madrid. *Envoy*'s web site claims that, as an instrument of the new evangelization, the magazine "explains it [the faith] intelligently, defends it charitably, and shares it effectively."[13] For the Catholic Right, catechesis on the "truths of the faith" lies at the heart of evangelization.

This catechetical evangelization consists of an invitation to Catholicism that comes from "all Catholics, not just the clergy and those in religious life."[14] Yet, evangelization is seen as taking place primarily at the individual, not communal, level. For example, one prepares individually to evangelize by reading the New Testament several times, "dipping" into the Old Testament, learning the catechism, and

---

12. Karl Keating, *12 Painless Ways to Evangelize* (El Cajon, Calif.: Catholic Answers, 1995), 3.

13. *Envoy Magazine* web site, www.envoymagazine.com.

14. "Catholic Answers Tour: Our Apostolate," www.catholic.com.

reading Catholic books, such as *Catholicism and Fundamentalism* by Karl Keating.[15] Though one can join with friends to plan an evangelization strategy for the area, the evangelical methods of the Catholic Right—as readers will see in the following paragraphs—typically lead members to evangelize individually.

Catholics are encouraged to direct their evangelization efforts at those with whom they are in personal relationship. They should "pick on one non-Catholic friend at a time" in their family, neighborhood, or work place.[16] For example, an *Envoy* reader writes of his experience evangelizing a Jewish co-worker who considered becoming Protestant. He gave her Catholic question-and-answer booklets in an attempt to bring her to Catholicism.[17] *Envoy* features several of these personal evangelization stories in each issue. They suggest that as more conservative Catholics evangelize, they reduce ecumenical and interreligious dialogue to an apologetic theology centered on defending the faith and conversion.

The Catholic Right's evangelization does not include a special emphasis on evangelizing the poor, as seen in a dearth of articles about the poor in more conservative periodicals. For example, a search of the *New Oxford Review* and *Catholic Answers* did not yield any articles about evangelizing the poor, and a recent article in *This Rock* stresses humanity's need for Christ's mercy over the need for social justice.[18] Conservative evangelical outreach too often overlooks the poor. At least one article focused on conversion of the local culture, noting that "missions to territories where people never heard of the gospel are old ways of evangelizing which no longer suffice."[19]

---

15. "Starting Out as an Apologist," www.catholic.com/library/starting_out_as_an_apologist.asp, May 25, 1996.

16. Ibid., 4.

17. Anonymous, "All in a Day's Work," *Envoy Magazine* 4.3 (March 1999), 2.

18. Jay Dunlap, "Social Justice and Divine Mercy," *This Rock* 12 (April 2001), 16–18.

19. Richard Rinaldi, "Cardinal George Focuses on 'New' in Evangelization," *National Catholic Register* 75 (October 24–30, 1999), 3.

The Catholic Right advocates an aggressive approach to converting individuals and society. They envision "mobilizing an army of new apostles" to bring the world to the Roman Catholic Church.[20] Their evangelization methods also reflect this aggressiveness. Keating recommends confronting door-to-door missionaries, writing to the editor when the press misrepresents the faith, calling radio talk shows, and distributing literature in a variety of places.[21] An editorial in the *New Oxford Review* encourages Catholics to evangelize door-to-door "like Mormons" because "setting a good example and affirming your faith is not enough."[22]

In order to achieve conversion, the new evangelization "requires a new catechesis as its 'engine.'"[23] In addition, the "new evangelization needs new apologetics."[24] Indeed, many on the Right seem to use the words evangelization and apologetics interchangeably. For instance, both *This Rock* and *Envoy* are self-described as magazines of "apologetics and evangelization." Patrick Madrid quotes Francis of Assisi's saying: "Evangelize always. When necessary, use words" at the beginning of a book entitled *Search and Rescue: How to Bring Your Family and Friends into — or Back into — the Catholic Church.*[25] Similarly, an article on the Catholic Answers web site, "Starting Out as an Apologist," provides step-by-step instructions on how to become an *apologist,* yet the closing sentence of the article states: "Keep this up long enough and you'll develop real skills as an *evangelist.*"[26] By equating evangelization, catechesis, and

---

20. "Shine Your Light," *National Catholic Register* 75 (October 24–30, 1999), 8.
21. Keating, *12 Painless Ways,* 7–11.
22. "Editorial," *New Oxford Review* 184 (March 12, 2001), 29–30.
23. Archbishop William Joseph Levada, "New Evangelization Requires a New Catechesis," *L'Osservatore Romano* 1543 (January 7, 1998), 11.
24. Archbishop Francis E. George, "New Evangelization Requires a New Catechesis," *L'Osservatore Romano* 1520 (December 10, 1997), 7.
25. (Manchester, New Hampshire: Sophia Institute Press, 2001).
26. Catholic Answers, "Starting Out," 4 (italics mine).

apologetics the purpose of evangelization becomes to defend the church and make people Catholics.

This "conversion and defense oriented" evangelization of the Catholic Right has its strengths. It encourages a trained laity willing to proclaim its beliefs. It centers on church teaching and therefore on the church as a universal community of believers. It makes excellent use of media resources to spread its message, as called for by the pope (*RM* 37, *EA* 72). However, its approach diverges from John Paul's new evangelization in essential elements.

First, the emphasis on evangelizing only in the personal realm neglects "the mission *ad gentes*" that John Paul II continues to proclaim (*RM* 37a, 62, 85; *EA* 74). Similarly, the Catholic Right's neglect of evangelizing the poor is not consonant with the new evangelization. By not specifically directing evangelization toward the poor, the Right ignores evangelizing "action on behalf of integral development and liberation from all forms of oppression" (*RM* 58). Action on behalf of justice and participation in the transformation of the world are not generally parts of its evangelical vision.

Another danger of a catechetical, apologetic evangelization is that it undervalues Christian witness and overemphasizes rational argument. A conservative journal claims that, "witness is not enough,"[27] yet John Paul II continues to proclaim that "witness is the first irreplaceable form of mission" (*RM* 42). Furthermore, intellect cannot create conversion, because "it is not simply a matter of thinking differently in an intellectual sense but of revising one's actions in light of the Gospel" (*EA* 26).

Most important for the Right, the church's catechism leads to Christ. However, John Paul asserts that Christ leads to the church. Experiencing Christ in one's heart leads one to encounter Jesus more fully in community and in the church (*EA* 68). This is an important distinction because "the kingdom of God is not a concept,

---

27. "All in a Day's Work," *Envoy Magazine* 4/3 (March 1999), 2.

a doctrine, or a program subject to free interpretation, but it is before all else a person with the face and name of Jesus of Nazareth" (*RM* 18). Though the "encounter with Christ has an essentially ecclesial dimension" (*EA* 68), the Catholic Right cannot replace Christology with ecclesiology as the central message of the church.

In these differences, one notes a divergence between the evangelization of the Catholic Right in the United States and John Paul II's new evangelization. But there is a similar divergence between the Catholic Right and Center.

The Catholic Center

While the new apologists represent the more conservative position on evangelization, the USCCB represents the Catholic Center, as does the Paulist National Catholic Evangelization Association, which is in service to the USCCB.[28] The bishops' pastoral letter, "Go and Make Disciples: A National Plan and Strategy for Catholic Evangelization in the U.S.," can serve as an example of a centrist evangelical model.[29] According to this letter, evangelization brings "the good news of Jesus into every human situation and seeks to convert individuals and society by the divine power of the Gospel itself."[30] From this centrist's perspective, Christ lies at the heart of evangelization.

"Go and Make Disciples" calls all Christians to proclaim the Word. This proclamation springs from parishes as they bring about in each parishioner an enthusiasm for the faith, for sacramental expression, and for the Catholic heritage. With the support of the parish, members continually renew their own faith. Through a constant inward reception of the gospel, an "outward address" arises,

---

28. Paulist National Catholic Evangelization Association web page, www.pncea.org.
29. "Go and Make Disciples: A National Plan and Strategy for Catholic Evangelization in the U.S.," *Origins* 22 (December 3, 1992), 423–32.
30. Ibid., 424.

directed to all non-Christians, but particularly "to inactive Catholics and the unchurched."[31] The new evangelization demands reevangelization.

The new evangelization also demands evangelization through ecumenical and interreligious dialogue. From this centrist perspective, ecumenical dialogue focuses on the unity of all Christians, not the conversion of all to Catholicism. Similarly, the pastoral letter states that though "the Lord gave us a message that is unique [and]…to know Jesus and belong to his Church is not the same as believing anything," interreligious dialogue does not proselytize or manipulate.[32] Thus the centrist impulse is to enter dialogue in order to forge bonds with others while maintaining the primacy of Christ and the Catholic Church.

The pastoral letter also maintains the primacy of evangelizing the poor. This is done by implementing Catholic social doctrine, serving parish neighborhoods, and questioning political and economic systems.[33] As the good news of the gospel grows, it will "overflow from each heart until the presence of God transforms all human existence."[34] In this way, parishes and their members will evangelize all of society.

To infuse individuals and society with the gospel, centrists advocate a businesslike evangelical approach that manifests itself in their methods of evangelization. For example, the Paulists have several parish-based mission programs such as Alpha for Catholics, Disciples in Mission, and Follow Me.[35] These programs are well-thought-out and comprehensive. "Disciples in Mission…integrates prayer, the Sunday liturgies, faith-sharing groups for adults and

---

31. Paulist National Catholic Evangelization Association web page, www.pncea.org.
32. "Go and Make Disciples," 425.
33. Ibid., 429–30.
34. Ibid., 424.
35. National Conference of Catholic Bishops web site, www.usccb.org/evangelization/programs.htm.

teens, catechesis, family activities, planning and follow up activities into a coherent, parish-wide experience of evangelization."[36] Another sign of the centrists' methodical approach is the structure of "Go and Make Disciples." It has three goals that revolve around the call to holiness, the call to welcome and invite, and the call to transform the world in Christ. Each goal is followed by hundreds of suggestions for implementation.

Despite the businesslike organization, the evangelization initiatives create a welcoming atmosphere. For example, Alpha for Catholics centers on informal discussions and dinners.[37] The parish evangelization programs convey friendship, attend to personal needs, and recognize both the spiritual and social elements of the Word.[38] Though evangelization sometimes means confronting society "like the prophets of old," centrists think that one typically encounters Christ through witness, friendship, and community. Through this fellowship, one then progresses to inquire about catechesis and formal initiation processes into the church.[39] Thus, the purpose of evangelization for centrists is to renew personal faith, invite the unchurched to participation in the community, and witness to the transformative power of Jesus Christ in society.

The personal and communal focus of centrist evangelization is a strength of the model. The root of evangelical activity is the parish—the local manifestation of the universal church. Additionally, parishes foster members' renewed relationship with Christ, which becomes the impetus for evangelization. Thus, Christ is at the core of evangelical outreach. John Paul II calls for each of these elements in his new evangelization.

---

36. "Disciples in Mission: An Evangelization Experience," www.disciplesinmission.org, May 5, 2000, 2.

37. "Alpha for Catholics," www.christlife.org.

38. Alvin Illig, "Evangelization in the 80's," in *Converts, Dropouts and Returnees,* Dean Hoge, ed. (New York: Pilgrim Press, 1981), 173–83.

39. "Go and Make Disciples," 424.

However, there are risks inherent to the centrist model of evangelization, which begins with personal renewal of faith. Parishes need to make certain that parishioners' personal renewal propels them to an outward proclamation and does not remain inwardly focused. Furthermore, an emphasis on evangelization in the local area can lead to a neglect of the mission *ad gentes*. Bishops need to "direct their fair share of resources" to the international community (*RM* 63). Similarly, emphasis on service must extend beyond the parish or diocesan boundaries. In short, "local churches, although rooted in their own people and their own culture, must always maintain an effective sense of the universality of the faith" (*RM* 85). Though evangelization efforts begin at the personal and parochial level, parish leaders need to make certain that evangelization does not end there.

The Catholic Left

While the Center focuses on evangelization in the ecclesial community, and the Catholic Right concentrates on apologetics and catechesis, the key element of evangelization for the Catholic Left is work toward reform and liberation. Call to Action, a group associated with the Catholic Left, writes that "to be a clearer sign and a better servant to God's global family, our church must reform its own structures....For the world's sake, let us make the church more faithful to its mission."[40] They equate successful completion of the church's mission with reform of the institution. Likewise, the group We Are Church in a "Proposed Constitution of the Catholic Church" states: "We hold that the Church's mission, grounded in the Gospel, is to proclaim and show forth Jesus' Good News...in individual and communal justice and love....Fundamental to the Church's mission are certain rights and

---

40. Call to Action web site, www.cta-usa.org/socialjustice.html.

responsibilities which pertain to all members."[41] The list of liberties due to all church members includes the right to participation in self-governance, the right to due process of law, the right to the accountability of chosen leaders, and the right to marry. Obviously, these "rights"—which We Are Church associates with the church's mission—would require significant reform within the church. Richard McBrien summarizes well the position of the Left when he writes that "to be concerned about the renewal and reform of the Church is to be concerned about mission as well."[42]

Another distinct, though related, perspective stems from Base Christian Communities (BCCs), which are at the core of the Catholic Left. Margaret Hebblethwaite, in *Base Christian Communities: An Introduction*, notes:

> The internal benefits of small Christian community are worthless unless there is also a missionary dimension. And that means that the middle-class members must go out, putting their gifts at the service of others who may not live in their locality and putting their gifts especially at the service of the poor.[43]

Hebblethwaite defines "missionary action" as service to the poor. Likewise, Leonardo Boff states that the Christian message of the BCCs "preaches not only resurrection, but the just quality of the temporal life of human beings."[44] From the perspective of the BCCs, evangelization's core component is action and service to the poor.

---

41. International Movement We Are Church web site, www.we-are-church.org/announcements/constit.htm.

42. Richard McBrien, "Some Say, 'Leave the Church Alone, Get Out There and Evangelize,'" *NCR* 36 (November 12, 1999), 21.

43. Margaret Hebblethwaite, *Base Christian Communities: An Introduction* (New York/Mahwah, N.J.: Paulist Press, 1994), 87.

44. Leonardo Boff, *Ecclesiogenesis: The Base Communities Reinvent the Church* (New York: Orbis Books, 1986), 38.

Thus, one can conclude that for the Catholic Left, evangelization means reform of the church and liberating action on behalf of the poor. However, this limited focus on reform and liberation can lead to a neglect of traditional evangelization associated with proclamation of the gospel and the explanation of Catholicism. For example, McBrien states:

> Some Christians assume a militant posture. They call for renewed efforts at "evangelization" understood not in the broad and comprehensive manner of Paul VI's 1975 apostolic exhortation *Evangelii nuntiandi*...but in the narrow sense of "making converts" or of bringing the "fallen away" Catholics back to the Church.[45]

Here, McBrien dismisses conversion and "reevangelization" as militant when in reality they are essential components of the church's evangelical outreach.

A survey of progressive authors and journals supports the critique that the Left largely ignores traditional evangelization. Evangelization itself, so central to the church's mission, is rarely mentioned. Richard McBrien's 1,186 page book *Catholicism* refers to *evangelization* only four times while the term *liberation theology* appears sixteen times.[46] Likewise, a search of *America* between 1994 and 2000 for the words *evangelize* or *evangelization* yields forty-eight articles while the words *justice* and *poor* produce 217 articles. A similar search of *Commonweal* reveals one article dealing with evangelization while it shows 115 articles relating to the poor.

Consistent with the notion that evangelization requires reform and liberation, the Left espouses a critical knowledge of those who are to be evangelized (that is, reformed or liberated). For instance, an

---

45. Richard P. McBrien, *Catholicism* (Minneapolis: Winston Press, 1980), 268.
46. Richard P. McBrien, *Catholicism: New Edition* (San Francisco: Harper, 1994).

article in *America* looks to the socioeconomic reasons for the prolif-eration of Protestant sects in Latin America.[47] In another *America* article, Andrew Greeley advocates using sociological data before evangelizing Catholics about sexual issues. He laments that "pro-moters of 'evangelization' campaigns don't feel they need to know anything about their targets."[48] Knowledge of those to be evangelized also stems from living among the people, as BCCs do.

One target of the Left's action-oriented, critical evangelization is the hierarchy. In Boff's words: "The bishop evangelizes the people and the people evangelize the bishop. Otherwise, who evangelizes the bishop?"[49] Similarly, an article in the liberal *National Catholic Reporter* acknowledges that priests evangelize the laity, but the article also asks the question: "What if he [the priest] needs evangelization?"[50] The Left makes it clear that evangelization of the hierarchy will pri-marily occur through reform of the church's unjust structures. Entering into ecumenical and interreligious dialogue can also affect church reform as Catholics simultaneously gain insight into other tra-ditions and religions as well as their own while working toward unity.

Of course, the primary targets of the Catholic Left's evangeliza-tion seem to be the poor because "…the word of God comes to man-ifestation as a factor for transformation, and for the liberation of the oppressed."[51] Just as evangelization of the hierarchy catalyzes into church reform, evangelization of the poor is incomplete without social and political action. For the evangelization of society can only occur through liberation from all oligarchal and patriarchal structures.

---

47. James Torrens, "A Fundamentalist Nicaragua," *America* 168 (January 16–23, 1993), 6–9.

48. Andrew Greeley, "Prospects for 'Evangelization'" *America* 178 (January 17–24, 1998), 8.

49. Boff, *Ecclesiogenesis*, 40.

50. Jeannette Batz, "The Best Place to Evangelize Culture Isn't from on High," *NCR* 35 (May 14, 1998), 18.

51. Boff, *Ecclesiogenesis*, 34.

The Left's evangelization of society begins with an approach that appeals to existential questions. Evangelization should begin, "not from the Creed, not from the catechism…but from the hunger for more than survival. Where Jesus started."[52] The evangelical methods of those on the Catholic Left support this existential approach. Their methods stress bearing witness to Christ by "being present to people and spending time with them."[53] They also advocate evangelizing by offering services like baby-sitting, tutorials for high-school equivalency exams, and exercise classes.[54] As mentioned, working for church and social reform is another method of evangelization. Thus, the purpose of the Left's new evangelization is to be present in the community and, through reform, to liberate humanity from oppressive structures.

The Left's preferential option for the poor is one of its strengths. Emphasizing justice for the poor dovetails with John Paul II's call to incorporate the church's social doctrine into evangelization (*EA* 54) while the BCCs correspond to the pope's summons "to form ecclesial communities and groups of a size that allow for true human relationships" (*EA* 41). Furthermore, the Left's dialogue with non-Catholics, like that advocated by John Paul II, is "a means of mutual knowledge and enrichment, and is not in opposition to the mission *ad gentes*" (*RM* 55).

However, a critique of the Catholic Left must include the extent to which it reduces the church's task or mission, and thus evangelization, to reform and liberation. In this narrowness, it is in danger of a one-sided humanizing and secularizing of the kingdom (cf. *RM* 17). Personal conversion and the name of Jesus must remain the center of

---

52. William J. O'Malley, "Hunger for the Connection," *America* 177 (October 18, 1997), 15.

53. Arthur Jones, "Evangelization Is a Challenge, Merry, Too," *NCR* 32 (July 12, 1996), 3.

54. Tim Unsworth, "Keeping Gyms Lighted May Keep Pews Full," *NCR* 32 (January 26, 1996), 18.

evangelization (*EA* 26; *RM* 44, 46). Furthermore, an unhealthy emphasis on church reform can lead people to forget that "the kingdom cannot be detached either from Christ or from the Church" (*RM* 18). And while interreligious dialogue should not be a cover for proselytism, it must "confirm the need for the Church, into which people enter through Baptism as through a door" (*RM* 55).

Another temptation of the Left's concern for justice is to politicize the church. Some liberation theologians, Boff for instance, argue that "Jesus was a hundred percent political."[55] Pope John Paul II rejects this approach. While "involvement in the political field is clearly a part of the vocation and activity of the lay faithful,...the Church can in no way be confused with the political community nor be tied to any political system" (*EA* 27). Evangelizing should not be identified with political affiliation.

While both the Catholic Left and John Paul advocate the centrality of liberation, their process of arriving at it differs. The Left's evangelization advocates reform that leads to liberation and development. For John Paul II, liberation and development begin with conversion. For him, it is "through the gospel message, [that] the Church offers a force for liberation which promotes development precisely because it leads to conversion of heart and of ways of thinking" (*RM* 59). The Catholic Left cannot offer a viable evangelical message unless it, too, is rooted in Christ.

An Authentic Catholic Evangelization

Thus, there are serious differences among the three approaches to evangelization. The Catholic Right defines it as an invitation to Catholicism, the Center as a proclamation of the good news of Jesus, and the Left as reforming action. Just as divisions among Christian denominations "damage the holy work of preaching the Gospel to

---

55. Boff, *Ecclesiogenesis*, 41.

every creature and are a barrier for many in their approach to faith" (RM 56), so, too, divisions in the Catholic evangelical message impede peoples' coming to Christ and the church. Therefore, Catholicism needs a unified approach to evangelization.

An authentic Catholic evangelization—one that is faithful to the 1971 Synod, Paul VI, and John Paul II—must have a kerygmatic witness to Jesus Christ as its central emphasis. If each of the three approaches we have considered maintained a kerygmatic witness that unites personal proclamation of the gospel with Christlike action as its evangelical focus, the Right would veer away from an exclusively ecclesiological emphasis, the Center would veer from an excessively inward focus, and the Left would avoid the reduction of proclamation to liberation and church reform. Simultaneously speaking of and living Christ must define Catholic evangelization.

In order to prepare for kerygmatic witness, all approaches need to advocate, as the centrists do, a constantly renewed relationship with Jesus Christ. Espousing a personal love of Christ as the basis for evangelization would correct the Right's emphasis on "right answers" while at the same time adjusting the Left's stress on reform and liberation. Love of Christ, not any narrow apologetic theology or program of social reform, should be the center of all Catholic evangelization efforts.

An authentic Catholic evangelization should direct this love of Christ, expressed through kerygmatic witness, to all sectors of society. Just as Christ befriended the wealthy and the poor, the righteous and the sinner, so, too, the Catholic evangelical message must reach all people. With this focus, the Right will move beyond evangelizing in personal relationships, the Center will move beyond evangelizing in the diocese, and the Left will move beyond evangelizing the hierarchy and the marginalized. An authentic Catholic evangelization involves all of these groups.

If authentic Catholic evangelization is kerygmatic witness to all people, rooted in love for Christ, then its purpose is to spread the Word and build the Body of Christ on earth. The Centrists' purpose of evangelization aligns closely with this vision of authentic Catholic evangelization. However, the Right's preoccupation with converting and defending as well as with the Left's overemphasis on ecclesial reform and liberation—to be present in the community and to liberate humanity from oppressive structures—seriously diverge from this vision.

Christ came to reconcile us to the Father and to one another. If Catholics cannot agree on a vision of evangelization that draws peoples to both God and greater community with each other, the church's evangelical efforts will continue to be frustrated.

Chapter 3

Evangelization in the Contemporary Catholic Church

Robert S. Rivers, C.S.P.

Sometimes in our lives, we do something for one set of reasons, and discover later more meaningful motives for our action. I had been a diocesan priest in Winona, Minnesota, for six years when I sought, and received, permission to join the Missionary Society of St. Paul the Apostle—more commonly known as the Paulist Fathers. I did this because I was looking for a greater level of community life and collaboration with my brother priests than I was able to find in the diocesan setting.

A year later, in 1976, I read Pope Paul VI's apostolic exhortation *On Evangelization in the Modern World (Evangelii nuntiandi)*, which had recently been promulgated, and I realized why I had become a Paulist. Evangelization had always been the work of the community, although we didn't call it that. The document gave new life to the historic Paulist mission, and as a newly professed Paulist, I felt called to carry out the work of evangelization.

The church has gone through a similar experience, with its discovery of evangelization as the deeper purpose of the Second Vatican

Council. Paul VI gave us this new interpretation of the Council in the opening paragraphs of *On Evangelization in the Modern World*. Since its promulgation in 1975, the entire church has been growing in its openness to evangelization as its essential mission. John Paul II, from the very beginning of his papacy, has repeatedly reaffirmed this vision of a missionary church.

Evangelization has come along at just the right time. It is a work of the Holy Spirit and was the very purpose of the Vatican Council. The renewal of Vatican II has brought much upheaval—which, in turn, resulted in a great need for evangelization. In this chapter, I will show how evangelization can be a remedy for that upheaval. I will also examine the pastoral implementation of evangelization: Is it in fact bringing new vigor to the church?

I. The Contemporary Context: A Church in Need of Evangelization

Vatican II opened the church to a wonderful experience of renewal, but also brought a great deal of upheaval. Alienation from the church, declining attendance at Sunday Mass, huge declines in the number of priests and religious, confusion and division over the church's teachings, significant levels of disaffiliation among young people, scandals of pedophilia—all of these are well-documented. I want to acknowledge the upheaval and take a closer look at it, for it provides the immediate context for contemporary Catholic evangelization in the United States.

This upheaval may well have occurred in some measure even if the Council never had taken place. The changes that happened in the United States in the late 1950s would certainly have had a significant impact on the Catholic Church. However, the decisions of the Council Fathers transformed the church's inner landscape and opened it to modernity in many different ways. Therefore, the

Council itself must be considered a catalyst for the upheaval. In ways most people would not have foreseen, the Council gave rise to theological controversy, divisions between conservatives and liberals, conflicts with magisterial authority, discrepancies between official policies and pastoral practices, and unresolved issues such as women's ordination—all of which have resulted in considerable turmoil.[1]

This is not to say that Catholics in the United States did not welcome the changes of the Vatican Council. As Thomas Rausch states in *Catholicism at the Dawn of the Third Millennium*: "For the vast majority of Catholics throughout the world, Vatican II now belongs to history, and the changes it introduced into Catholic life are taken for granted....In more technical language, the council has been received by the Church."[2]

However, we face a paradox today: If there is widespread acceptance of the teachings of the Council, it also produced notable losses. Inactive Catholics continue to make up the second largest denomination in the country: sixteen-to-eighteen million people and growing. The trend among the post-Vatican II generation of Catholics is toward lower levels of participation and declining levels of attachment to the church as an institution.[3]

Young adult Catholics, because they represent the future, constitute a special area of concern. There is substantial evidence that large numbers of them, while claiming to be Catholic, do not in fact practice their faith or have a strong sense of Catholic identity. The question legitimately arises as to whether they can and will pass their faith on to the next generation. Furthermore, what kind of Catholic

---

1. See Charles R. Morris, *American Catholic* (New York: Random House, 1997). For a specific example of the division in the area of liturgy, see Rembert Weakland, "The Liturgy as Battlefield," *Commonweal* 129/1 (January 11, 2002), 10–15.

2. Thomas P. Rausch, *Catholicism at the Dawn of the Third Millennium* (Collegeville, Minn.: The Liturgical Press, 1996), 204.

3. William V. D'Antonio, James D. Davidson, Dean R. Hoge, Katherine Meyer, *American Catholics* (Walnut Creek, Lanham, N.Y./Oxford: AltaMira Press, 2001), 21–23; 28–29; 36–37; 47–50; 66–67; 85–86.

identity will they pass on? Studies of post-Vatican II generations and their relationship to the church are not reassuring.[4] For example, this generation is noted for its skepticism about institutions in general and its tendency to evaluate things from a subjective viewpoint, rather than from objective criteria.

In *Young Adult Catholics: Religion in the Culture of Choice*, Dean R. Hoge and his associates identify the major characteristic of the assimilated Catholic of the postmodern era. Freedom of choice and the autonomy of the individual are pillars of modern U.S. culture. Not surprisingly, post-Vatican II Catholics have been profoundly affected by these values. As a result, they tend to have a weaker attachment to the church.[5] The "pick and choose" character of the post-Vatican II generation's approach to doctrines and morals is well-known. They do not look to the church for guidance in sexual morality. While there is significant agreement on major doctrines, there is also significant dissent in areas like women's ordination, married priests, and aspects of religious practice (Sunday Mass attendance, confession, and the financial support of the parish). Many observers have noted that this generation, while admiring the Holy Father immensely, feels no great need to obey him. Yet, they often speak of themselves as spiritual, and define their religion as being a "good person."[6]

William V. D'Antonio, James D. Davidson, Dean R. Hoge, and Katherine Meyer in *American Catholics* show declining levels of attachment to the Catholic Church at the belief level. The graph below compares responses from the years 1987, 1993, and 1999 to

---

4. Dean R. Hoge, William D. Dinges, Mary Johnson, Juan L. Gonzales, Jr., *Young Adult Catholics: Religion in the Culture of Choice* (Notre Dame, Ind.: University of Notre Dame, 2001), 218–30; also see James T. Fisher, "Young American Catholics: Who Are They and What Do They Want?" *Commonweal* 129/1 (November 23, 2001), 10–15.

5. Hoge et al., 218–30.

6. Ibid., 33.

the following question: "Please tell me if you think a person can be a good Catholic without performing these actions or affirming these beliefs":[7]

	1987 %	1993 %	1999 %
Without believing that Jesus physically rose from the dead	*	*	23
Without believing that in the Mass, the bread and wine actually become the body and blood of Jesus	*	*	38
Without obeying the church hierarchy's teaching regarding abortion	39	56	53
Without donating time or money to help the poor	44	52	56
Without donating time or money to help the parish	*	57	60
Without their marriage being approved by the Catholic Church	51	61	67
Without obeying the church hierarchy's teaching on divorce and remarriage	57	62	64
Without obeying the church hierarchy's teaching on birth control	66	73	71
Without going to church every Sunday	70	73	76

7. D'Antonio et al., *American Catholics*, 43; an asterisk (*) means that question was not asked in 1987 and/or 1993.

Recent research on American Catholics, especially young adults, shows overall a weakening connection to the church and a reduced level of participation in church life. This is the contemporary context within which the church in the United States seeks to undertake its mission of evangelization.

II. Evangelization:
A Response to the Contemporary Context

It is not widely realized that evangelization was the principal theme of the Second Vatican Council. After all, there are no documents on evangelization. Yet Avery Dulles, now Cardinal Dulles, in a 1995 speech points to the opening of *On Evangelization in the Modern World*, which sums up the objectives of the Council as follows: "to make the Church of the twentieth century ever better fitted for proclaiming the Gospel to the people of the twentieth century."[8] In effect, Dulles says, in doing this Paul VI gave a new interpretation to the Council.[9] This evangelizing purpose is also expressed in a speech that John XXIII made prior to the Council in which he stated: "The purpose of the Council is, therefore, evangelization."[10]

Evangelization, then, is not a new program. It is a way of being church. A great deal of what we have been doing in these last forty years of renewal—focusing more deeply on scripture, enriching the liturgy, working for justice for all—is evangelization. Paul VI defined evangelization in the broadest possible terms. In fact, he was concerned that we accept no partial or fragmentary definition that would diminish the complexity, dynamism, and richness of evangelization.[11]

---

8. Paul VI, *On Evangelization in the Modern World* (Boston: Pauline Books and Media, 1975), no. 2.

9. *Origins*, 25/23 (November 23, 1995), 397–400.

10. Giuseppe Alberigo and Joseph A. Komonchak, *History of Vatican II*, vol. 1 (Maryknoll, N.Y.: Orbis/Leuven: Peeters, 1995), 439.

11. *On Evangelization in the Modern World*, no. 17.

This is one of the strengths of Catholic evangelization: It cannot be reduced to one-on-one conversion, door-to-door visitation, or televangelism.

However, if everything is evangelization, nothing is evangelization. Clearly, this is a way of being church that has a certain edge. What is this edge? Evangelization challenges all baptized persons to a conversion to Christ, by living their faith fully, sharing it freely, and living these gospel values in the world. It is not enough to live our faith in isolation, to keep it to ourselves. Evangelization thus provides a new lens through which we can view our Catholic faith. That lens is threefold: spiritual renewal, missionary activity, and action for justice in the world.[12]

One might even say that the Second Vatican Council was the church evangelizing itself! Catholic culture prior to the Council was clerical, authoritarian, legalistic, moralistic, and ritualistic. This culture powerfully impacted the way that Catholics pursued their spiritual lives. Often, spirituality was very narrowly defined. One of the great achievements of Vatican II was that it reaffirmed that *all* baptized persons are called to holiness, and that the laity's call was not to a monastic holiness but to a secular holiness, based on its proper vocation in the world.

Similarly, the missionary consciousness of pre-Vatican II Catholics defined the missions as Africa, the Fiji Islands, China, and India. The missionaries were the Jesuits, the Franciscans, the Maryknoll Fathers and Sisters, and the Missionaries of Africa. Vatican II, however, asserted that the entire church was by its very nature missionary.[13] Wherever we are is the mission, and we are the missionaries.

12. The three essential characteristics of evangelization correspond to the three Goals of *Go and Make Disciples: A National Plan of Strategy for Catholic Evangelization in the United States* (Washington, D.C.: United States Catholic Conference of Bishops, 1993).

13. Decree on the Church's Missionary Activity, no. 2, *The Basic Sixteen Documents of Vatican II: Constitutions, Decrees, Declarations*, Austin Flannery, ed. (Northport, N.Y.: Costello Publishing Co., 1996), 814.

Just as Vatican II expanded our understanding of the universal call to holiness and missionary awareness, so it expanded our understanding of social justice. The years after the Council saw a growth in our awareness of the need to address the structures of society, as well as to rectify individual instances of injustice.

Thus evangelization is an integral but unfinished part of the renewal of Vatican II. If the church will carry out that renewal agenda in its explicit evangelizing dimensions, this will remedy much of the upheaval we face and will place the church in a powerful position to be the light of the gospel to the nations, as the Council originally intended.

I would like now to look at four areas of church life in which evangelization can help us respond to the current situation.

From Fragmentation to Unity

Pope Paul VI's *On Evangelization in the Modern World* states that "evangelizing all peoples constitutes the essential mission of the Church…it is in fact the grace and vocation proper to the Church, her deepest identity. She exists in order to evangelize."[14] In other words, evangelization is not one program among a host of possibilities; it is the umbrella under which all ministries are carried out. Everything we do must be seen as evangelization.

However, this was not really understood when we first began trying to carry out the Council's renewal agenda. We expended a lot of energy implementing separate aspects of the renewal in an isolated fashion. Often, we began with segments of the liturgical renewal. We also concentrated heavily on equipping the baptized to carry out their rightful ministry. Social justice became a central concern in the parish. Catechesis, originally limited to schools and religious education programs, grew to include the family, youth, and young adults.

---

14. *On Evangelization in the Modern World*, no. 14.

The result is that parishes have become very busy places; they seems to follow a philosophy that "more is better."

Sometimes this multiplication of ministries is accompanied by compartmentalization and a harmful "turfism." We see ministers focusing on one area of ministry, at the expense of the whole. Repeatedly, one encounters situations where the left hand does not know (or always care) what the right hand is doing. Evangelization, once it is understood as the essential mission of the church, has a unifying power to break down both turfism and excessive compartmentalization in ministry.

For example, evangelization can have a salutary effect on the role of catechesis in the church. Today, there is a growing divide between Catholic schools and parishes. Many parishes find themselves sponsoring and supporting schools with an increasingly large population of families of inactive Catholics or people with no church family. And many school families direct their primary loyalty to the school, rather than to the parish. A mutual distrust and lack of support often result.

However, the *General Directory for Catechesis* makes it very clear that catechesis is an essential moment in the overall ministry of evangelization.[15] So we now have a firm basis for establishing a new unity between school and parish, under the overall ministry of evangelization. The purpose of the parish and school is the same: evangelization.

From Maintenance to Mission

One Sunday, an elderly couple came up to me after Mass and said: "Father, all this talk about evangelization is fine. But while you are out taking care of *them*, who is going to take care of *us?*"

---

15. *General Directory for Catechesis* (Washington, D.C.: United States Catholic Conference, 1997), no. 59.

Many parishes are maintenance-oriented because their parishioners have a consumer consciousness.[16] Influenced by our consumer culture, they come to church to get something, and they expect the leadership to provide it. These good people have little missionary awareness. Parishes end up spending a lot of time and energy serving them, the people who are present, rather than reaching out to those who are absent.

But this is not what we hear in scripture. Jesus said to his listeners: "Those who are well do not need a physician, but the sick do. I did not come to call the righteous but sinners" (Mark 2:17). At the end of all the gospels, a missionary mandate accompanies the resurrection appearances. The most dramatic is in Matthew: "Go, make disciples of all nations…" (28:16–20).

In keeping with this mandate, canon law emphasizes that the pastor is responsible for everyone within the parish boundaries, not just the people who regularly come to church. Canon 528 states: "The pastor…is to make every effort with the aid of the Christian faithful, to bring the gospel message also to those who have ceased practicing their religion or who do not profess the true faith."[17]

But the need to reach out beyond our boundaries is more than a mandate; it is a practical necessity. In his monumental work, *Transforming Mission*, David Bosch comments that movements, in order to survive, have to institutionalize themselves. But institutions, in order to stay vital, have to stay in touch with the original inspiring character of their founding as a movement.[18] For the church, this means that we have to constantly reawaken ourselves to the boundary-breaking, all-inclusive character of Jesus' original mission of salvation for all. Parishes in America "should be distinguished by their

---

16. Patrick J. Brennan, *Re-Imagining the Parish* (New York: Crossroad, 1991), 10.

17. *Code of Canon Law: Latin-English Edition* (Washington, D.C.: Canon Law Society of America, 1983), 201.

18. David J. Bosch, *Transforming Mission: Paradigm Shifts in Theology of Mission* (Maryknoll, N.Y.: Orbis, 1996), 52–54.

missionary spirit, which leads them to reach out to those who are far away."[19] This is how they stay vital.

It is also how they stay healthy. Organizational development tells us that healthy organizations are those that have a clear sense of mission. Could it be true that clarity about and steady focus on our outward-reaching mission provide the healthiest context from which to deal with our internal problems? In adopting a missionary rather than a maintenance approach, parishes are not only being faithful to the mandate of Christ, but they also might find a remedy for the malaise that comes from excessive focus on their internal affairs.

From Blindness to Conversion

We human beings are like fish living in the ocean. We are largely oblivious to the culture that surrounds us and how it affects us. Ronald Rolheiser speaks about how many of us in the dominant culture are impacted in ways we don't perceive by narcissism, pragmatism, and unbridled restlessness.[20] The figure of the blind beggar Bartimaeus (Mark 10: 46–52) is often regarded as a foil for the disciples. They, too, are blind, only they don't realize it. Bartimaeus, though, is ready to throw off the cloak of fear and come to Jesus so that he might see—and thus we may view him as a model disciple.

I believe that God has made us with a powerful desire for truth, but also with a considerable capacity for self-delusion. We constantly need to have our eyes opened, so we can see things as they really are *(contemplatio)*. This is the ongoing struggle to conversion, and we are all called to it.

Conversion to the gospel of Jesus Christ is the heart of evangelization; it is the core of the message we bring to the world. If we

---

19. John Paul II, Apostolic Exhortation, *The Church in America* (Washington, D.C.: United States Conference of Catholic Bishops, 1999), no. 41.

20. Ronald Rolheiser, *The Shattered Lantern: Rediscovering a Felt Presence of God* (New York: Crossroad, 1994), 28–52.

actively open ourselves to the conversion power of the gospel by proclaiming it to all people, including ourselves, in every possible situation, allowing it to function as a two-edged sword cutting through to
the bone of the human situation, we will indeed be changed.

This transformation can be brought about only by the power of
the Holy Spirit who is the principal agent of evangelization. Only the
Spirit can change hearts. Only the Spirit can lead us to ask ourselves
the question: "What do I need to change?"—rather than pointing a fin-
ger at the other. There is nothing quite so humbling and salutary in the
body of Christ as the humble admission of our own need to change.

From Rugged Individualism to Solidarity

Goal III of the U.S. bishops' plan for Catholic evangelization,
Go and Make Disciples, states: "to foster gospel values in our society,
promoting the dignity of the human person, the importance of the
family, and the common good of our society so that our nation may
continue to be transformed by the saving power of Jesus Christ."[21] In
effect, Goal III focuses on the social justice aspect of evangelization.
The document goes on: "The fruit of evangelization is changed lives
and a changed world—holiness and justice, spirituality and peace."[22]
We are not content simply to change individuals; we want to change
the world.

Moreover, we participate in the transformation of culture not
by assuming that the church has all the answers, but knowing that
the Holy Spirit is at work in the church and in the world, bringing
about the fulfillment of God's plan for God's creation. We are
engaged in a process of discerning where and how gospel values are
actually at work and in place in the world and in the church. The
document on adult faith formation, Our Hearts Were Burning within

---

21. Go and Make Disciples, 8.
22. Ibid., 3.

Us, describes this challenge by saying: "Inculturation is a process of mutual enrichment between the Gospel and culture."[23]

So there is a powerful sense of solidarity with the world, a growing together with the world as we seek to bring God's creation to its fulfillment. In particular, this solidarity must be with the world's poor, those without recourse. Without a doubt, the widening division between the rich and the poor continues to be one of the most serious social justice issues facing our world. If we wish to wipe out the breeding ground of terrorism in a post-September 11 world, we could do no better than to start with this issue. God has linked us together, so that one part of the world cannot thrive while another languishes. Our world is full of pain that arises out of our inability to find effective ways to live out the virtue of solidarity.

The *Catechism of the Catholic Church* describes solidarity as a social charity that is a direct demand of human and Christian brotherhood.[24] In St. Paul's words: "None of us lives to ourselves and none of us dies to ourselves" (Rom 14:7). Solidarity is the conviction that humanity is rooted in a common origin as a family and bonded together in an obligation of mutual charity. Solidarity is the conviction that human existence is coexistence.[25] This is not a solo trip. We are required to live not just for ourselves, but in service of the common good. Evangelization is profoundly personal, inevitably communal, and ineluctably social in its perspective, and solidarity is the finest expression of this social perspective.

---

23. *Our Hearts Were Burning within Us* (Washington, D.C.: United States Conference of Catholic Bishops, 1999), 28.

24. *Catechism of the Catholic Church* (New York: Paulist Press, 1994), no. 1939.

25. Richard. P. McBrien, *Catholicism: New Edition* (San Francisco: Harper, 1994), 166.

III. Pastoral Implementation

Recently, evangelization has risen on the priority lists of parishes and arch/dioceses across the country. Many arch/dioceses have evangelization coordinators and many parishes have evangelization committees. Evangelization programs are more common. Catholics are beginning to grasp that evangelization is not something foreign to their faith, but lies at the core of what it means to be Catholic.

However, evangelization has not yet truly taken its rightful place as the central mission of the church. Two basic challenges need to be addressed before this can happen. First, as mentioned earlier, many parishes and arch/dioceses are stuck in a maintenance mode: A good deal of their energy is spent on those who are already present. There is little missionary awareness on the part of either the leadership or the people. We need to get beyond this maintenance orientation.

The second challenge, not unrelated to the first, is that evangelization is not perceived as the *essential* mission of the church—again, either by the leadership or the people. Rather, it is seen as one priority among many. Often, it is viewed as a program that can be assigned to and implemented by an already existing committee. It is not understood as a way of being church.

For example, in the parish evangelization may become a committee of the parish council and a program to be carried out by this committee. That is like entrusting ushers with the task of creating a welcoming parish! Evangelization must be the work of the whole parish. It cannot be carried out by a committee. There is a legitimate function for an evangelization committee, but it is as a catalyst, a resource, and a model for evangelizing activities. It cannot "do" evangelization for parish members; that is taking from them a call and a responsibility that belong to everyone.

At the arch/diocesan level, evangelization often becomes a temporary priority in its overall pastoral agenda. It is the number one priority—until it is replaced by stewardship or a fund-raising campaign.

Or sometimes evangelization is chosen as the focus of an arch/diocese for a theme year, only to be followed by something else the next year. For the most part, we have not yet fully understood what it means in our pastoral planning to make evangelization the essential mission of the church, something that underlies and animates all our activities and programs.

Pastoral Planning from an Evangelizing Perspective

Putting evangelization at the center of our pastoral agenda was clearly the intention of the bishops when they wrote *Go and Make Disciples*. This plan and strategy was meant to be used as an effective tool to align parish resources, parish activities, and parishioner energies with three evangelization goals: to live our faith fully, to share it freely with others, and to transform the world in Christ. There is some evidence that this is beginning to happen.[26]

There is a way to overcome both of the obstacles listed above — the maintenance orientation and the perception of evangelization as one priority among many. It is to adopt an effective pastoral planning process that puts evangelization squarely at its heart as the essential mission of the church. While *Go and Make Disciples* presumes such a planning process for the implementation of its goals, this is easier said than done. Dioceses and parishes need lots of practical assistance as they undertake this effort. It requires a change in the way that we carry out our day-to-day ministry.[27]

---

26. The Paulist National Catholic Evangelization Association (PNCEA) has been working with thirty-three arch/dioceses in a formation process called *Disciples in Mission: An Evangelization Experience*. The purpose of *Disciples in Mission* is to assist arch/dioceses in implementing *Go and Make Disciples*. The process has proven effective thus far.

27. *Disciples in Mission* engages the parish in an initial, elementary planning process focused on goals. A lot more is required in order to make a parish truly evangelization-driven. The PNCEA is coming out with a much more sophisticated planning process to help parishes make evangelization the essential mission of the parish.

Turning an Evangelizing Lens on All Parish Ministries

Because Catholic evangelization is comprehensive in nature — it is a way of being church — many parishes have found an effective strategy in simply applying an evangelizing lens to all their current ministries. There is no need to begin a new program. We can simply look at what we are already doing and ask: How would we do these differently if we were using an evangelizing perspective? The answer is that by sharpening the spiritual renewal component, heightening the missionary outreach, and increasing the social justice impact of these ministries, we give them an evangelizing dimension.

Thus, parishes have found that the Sunday liturgy can become significantly more evangelizing through this strategy. If they focus on things such as the quality of the preaching and the way the Eucharist is celebrated, then the liturgy becomes more welcoming to strangers, has more power to convert, and better enhances missionary consciousness. Catholic schools and catechetical programs can become more evangelizing, if they pastor their inactive Catholics as an essential part of their work. They can increase the outreach power of their schools and catechetical programs by making evangelization central rather than peripheral to their efforts. Frank DeSiano, C.S.P., and Susan Blum-Gerding have written a book to help parishes equip their ministers in this approach to ministerial activities.[28]

Multicultural Awareness

Andrew Greeley noted some years ago that the Catholic Church was losing sixty-thousand Hispanics a year, people who had stopped actively practicing their faith.[29] The recent study, *Young Adult*

---

28. Susan Blum-Gerding and Frank DeSiano, C.S.P., *Lay Ministers, Lay Disciples: Evangelizing Power in the Parish* (New York: Paulist Press, 1999).

29. Andrew M. Greeley, "Defection Among Hispanics," *America* (July 30, 1988), 61–62; "Defection Among Hispanics (Updated)," *America* (Sept. 27, 1997), 12–13.

Catholics, somewhat surprisingly showed fewer losses among Hispanics than one might expect. However, the study was based on Catholics who were already confirmed and may have a significant bias from that point of view. In any case, in order to respond to a situation of huge losses, local parishes must find ways to become multicultural churches. Because this issue is being addressed elsewhere in this book, I will simply note in passing how important this is at the parish and diocesan levels, not only for Hispanics, but for all cultural groups.

Parish Structures and Operations

Another comprehensive approach to parish evangelization should be mentioned. Having certain parish structures and operations in place and functioning effectively gives a parish a powerful platform from which to carry out its evangelizing activities. I will simply mention them; their evangelization impact should be fairly obvious:

- a fully functioning RCIA with maximum parish participation
- parishwide, small faith-sharing communities
- regular parish visitations
- an evangelization committee

Parish Outreach Programs

As parishes become more actively missionary, they will need tools to help them effectively carry out their evangelizing activities. This is particularly true when we move beyond inactive Catholics to outreach to people with no church family. How do we reach out to people who have no history of involvement with the church, no Christian background, or may come from an anti-Christian background? Not much has been done in the Catholic Church in this area.[30]

---

30. *Alpha* is an evangelization program originally designed to reach out to the unchurched. It had its beginnings in the Anglican Church in central London, Holy

There are a number of programs to help parishes reach out to inactive Catholics. Oftentimes, this is most effectively done in collaboration with neighboring Catholic parishes. Most of these programs have developed successful formats for contacting inactive Catholics, for engaging them in a reconciliation or healing process, and for enabling them to resume their rightful place in the church. The USCCB Committee on Evangelization has published a resource directory, titled, A *Time to Listen...A Time to Heal*,[31] which lists many of them.

Studies show that inactive Catholics are very open to an invitation to return to the active practice of their faith.[32] The reasons they leave are myriad. Many times, they feel that the church doesn't really care; they don't feel missed. Sometimes, they have felt unwelcome. Sometimes, they are angry and alienated because of some particular experience with the church. Sometimes, it is only that they have moved and haven't become connected to a church in their new location. In any case, what is clear is that a genuine invitation is sometimes all it takes to bring an inactive Catholic back to the practice of the faith.

Conclusion

I have based my exploration of evangelization in the contemporary Catholic Church on the premise that evangelization is an integral part of the renewal of Vatican II. That renewal, in addition

---

Trinity Brompton, and is widely available in the United States. See Kristina Cooper, "The A, B and C of Alpha," *The Tablet* (February 24, 1996), 258; Ruth Gledhill, "The Magnet of Alpha," *The Tablet* (June 27, 1998), 838–41.

31. A *Time to Listen...A Time to Heal* (Washington, D.C.: United States Conference of Catholic Bishops, 1999).

32. George Gallup, *The Unchurched American* (Washington, D.C.: Paulist National Catholic Evangelization Association, 1988); for summary information, see the pamphlet *Another Look at the Catholic Faith* (Washington, D.C.: Paulist National Catholic Evangelization Association, 1992).

to being a great blessing, has brought an upheaval, which can be remedied by continuing to implement the unfinished, more explicit evangelizing agenda of the Council. Finally, I have examined some of the current efforts at implementation.

In the period from the Second Vatican Council to the Jubilee Year, the church was given the great grace of appropriating in our time evangelization as its essential mission. Beginning with the new millennium, we are being given the grace of systematically implementing it. In many ways, the fruits of that effort have yet to be seen.

Chapter 4

Evangelization and Liturgy

Thomas P. Rausch, S.J.

What role might liturgy play in the efforts of contemporary Roman Catholics to make their church more evangelical? There is a twofold problem here. First of all, most Catholics are not very familiar with the language of evangelization and tend to associate it more with conservative Protestantism. Second, I suspect that few Catholics grasp how powerful an instrument for evangelization their liturgy is. Yet, Pope John Paul II has explicitly linked evangelization with liturgy and most liturgical scholars recognize that liturgy is itself evangelical. This chapter will explore the relationship between liturgy and evangelization. Then, in an effort to illustrate the argument in concrete and practical terms, we will look at three successful parishes where worship has played a key role in developing a vital, evangelical community life.

Evangelization and Liturgy

Pope John Paul's explicit linking of evangelization and liturgy would probably be surprising to many Catholics. But he has done so repeatedly. In 1988, he linked his call for a new evangelization to a renewal of church life. "Without doubt a mending of the Christian fabric of society is urgently needed in all parts of the world. But for this to come about what is needed is to first remake the Christian fabric of the ecclesial community itself present in these countries and nations."[1] In describing the comprehensive or total evangelization he envisions to the Puerto Rican bishops during their 1988 *ad limina* visit, he said: "Such a total evangelization will naturally have its highest point in an intense liturgical life which will make the parishes living ecclesial communities."[2]

In his *Ecclesia in America,* an apostolic letter delivered in the course of a 1999 pastoral visit to Mexico, John Paul again emphasized the role of the liturgy in the church's evangelical mission.[3] Chapter 4 especially stresses the paths to communion, symbolized by the church (no. 33) and brought about through the sacraments, with their opportunities for evangelization and catechesis, calling special attention to the importance of Christian initiation (no. 34). The pope points to the Sunday celebration of the Eucharist as another opportunity for preaching and catechesis (no. 35), stressing that the bishops must ensure that the communion it effects and symbolizes must be promoted by all members of the church. The bishops should awaken in the faithful a missionary consciousness (no. 36), as well as a willingness to assume responsibility for developing bonds with local churches in other areas of America through education, the exchange of information, fraternal ties, projects involving cooperation, and joint intervention in questions of greater importance, especially those affecting the poor (no. 37).

The pope has a keen sense of how the liturgy brings the mysteries of the faith together in symbolic form and relates them to everyday life. However, I suspect that the average Catholic would have trouble seeing the connection between liturgy and evangelization. For most of

---

1. John Paul II, "The Vocation and the Mission of the Lay Faithful in the Church and in the World," December 30, 1988 (Washington, D.C.: United States Catholic Conference, n.d.), 96.

2. *L'Osservatore Romano* (English ed.), 49 (December 5, 1988), 14.

3. John Paul II, *Ecclesia in America, Origins* 28/33 (1999).

them, evangelization means preaching, missionary work, going door-to-door to invite others to a new relationship with Christ. Evangelization is about bringing people to church; it is not what takes place in church. Stanley Hauerwas once said something similar from a Protestant perspective when he pointed to the difference between a revival and church: "You 'got saved' in the tent. Worship was what you did in the church. Evangelism was what you did in the tent."[4] I suspect that many Catholics, however unfamiliar with the tent tradition, would still judge the average, nonliturgical Protestant service as more "evangelical" than Sunday Mass, not to mention the new phenomenon of the "seeker churches," whose easy informality and "Jesus rock" music is designed to draw in the unchurched.

Yet scholars as diverse as Don Saliers, Regis Duffy, Mary Catherine Hilkert, and Hauerwas seem to echo the pope in arguing that liturgy is itself evangelical.[5] Duffy argues from Vatican II's Constitution on the Liturgy (no. 2) that it is through the liturgy that the faithful are enabled to express in their lives and manifest to others the mystery of Christ.[6] Hilkert writes that "Christians are both challenged and enabled by the liturgy to reform their lives, their society, and their church so that they might more deeply reflect the gospel of Jesus."[7]

But does this really happen? In a collection of essays evaluating a 1988 study of liturgical renewal in fifteen middle-class U.S. parishes, a number of the contributors raised questions about the relation between Sunday liturgy and daily life. Aidan Kavanagh

---

4. Stanley M. Hauerwas, "Worship, Evangelism, Ethics: On Eliminating the 'And,'" in *Liturgy and the Moral Self: Humanity at Full Stretch Before God*, E. Byron Anderson and Bruce T. Morrill, eds. (Collegeville, Minn.: The Liturgical Press, 1998), 95.

5. Ibid. Hauerwas credits Saliers with helping Methodists see that worship is evangelism, with its particular ability to shape the affections.

6. Regis Duffy, *An American Emmaus: Faith and Sacrament in the American Church* (New York: Crossroad, 1995), 142.

7. Mary Catherine Hilkert, *Naming Grace: Preaching and the Sacramental Imagination* (New York: Contiuuum, 1997), 65.

found the "gathering rites" of welcome and hospitality that had developed in many parishes more reflective of middle-class culture and a "therapeutic" ecclesiology. "There is no prayer or Godward direction in this new 'rite of gathering'; it is a set of activities not ritually very different from the same procedures used when persons of middle-class society gather for any purpose."[8] Monika Hellwig welcomed the new involvement of the laity in the liturgy but questioned the sense that the real business of the church was liturgical worship, while "healing, reconciliation, and the service of practical human needs" was "for those with that particular charism or inclination."[9] John Baldovin commented on a tendency to look to liturgy for immediate gratification and a sense of community: "Overattention to intimacy and warmth also inhibits worshipers from experiencing sacramental action as God's gift rather than their own creation."[10]

Can an intense liturgical life transform parishes into communities of reconciliation and mission, and what might that mean in a North American context? How can the liturgy evangelize us as worshipers? Would we be more engaged as disciples of Jesus if we really saw blessing ourselves with holy water on entering a church or taking part in the rite of sprinkling as a renewal of our baptismal vows? How many Catholics today could even explain those vows? What if the penitential rite became for each of us a real confession of sins? Would we be more attentive to social justice if we brought forward with our gifts food for the hungry in our communities? Would we be

---

8. Aidan Kavanagh, "Reflections on the Study from the Viewpoint of Liturgical History," in *The Awakening Church: Twenty-five Years of Liturgical Renewal*, Lawrence J. Madden, ed. (Collegeville, Minn.: The Liturgical Press, 1992), 87.

9. Monika Hellwig, "Twenty-five Years of a Wakening Church: Liturgy and Ecclesiology," in *The Awakening Church*, 66.

10. John F. Baldovin, "Pastoral Liturgical Reflections on the Study," in *The Awakening Church*, 104. See Bruce T. Morrill's review of these and other essays in his *Anamnesis as Dangerous Memory: Political and Liturgical Theology in Dialogue* (Collegeville, Minn.: The Liturgical Press, 2000), 5–16.

able to better articulate our faith if we recited the creed with more attention? Would we be more moved to seek reconciliation with those we've injured or with others from whom we've become estranged if we saw the sign of peace as something more than a time of greeting friends or really understood that the Eucharist is the basic sacrament of reconciliation? How can we fail to learn the lesson of humble service when we participate in the washing of feet on Holy Thursday? And what if we really understood ourselves communally as the body of Christ for the world?

Liturgy, Evangelization, and Parish Life

In an earlier day in the United States, people were to a considerable degree shaped and formed by the neighborhood communities in which they grew up and lived. When their neighborhoods were still largely ethnic enclaves, church, ethnic background, and the extended family were all part of a common culture. But that kind of social cohesion has long ago disappeared. The old neighborhood is gone. Andrew Greeley has observed that parishes "are the religious counterparts of neighborhoods,"[11] or perhaps it might be more accurate to say that they are often the successor to the neighborhoods we once had.

In many parts of the United States today, it is not uncommon for people to "shop" for a parish that meets their needs. According to Archbishop Rembert Weakland, those that represent the largest group in his archdiocese of Milwaukee are looking for vital parishes with good liturgies and preaching, effective educational programs, and an ability to introduce their children to the riches of the faith.[12] They also want a sense of community that counterbalances the

---

11. Andrew M. Greeley and Mary Greeley Durkin, *How to Save the Catholic Church* (New York: Viking, 1984), 167.

12. Rembert G. Weakland, "Reflections for Rome," *America* 178/13 (1998), 12–13.

individualism, disconnectedness, and isolation of our contemporary secular culture.

The statement that good liturgy and good preaching make for an effective parish is frequently heard; it has become almost a slogan. But what are the signs or indicators of a parish's vitality that might be considered signs of an evangelical effectiveness? I'd like to outline some criteria and then consider three very diverse Los Angeles parishes, each of which places a high priority on liturgy and preaching.[13] One is situated in an affluent west-side neighborhood, another in the decaying South Central part of the city, and one in an East Los Angeles housing project.

St. Monica's, an upscale parish in Santa Monica, California, is known throughout the archdiocese of Los Angeles as the premier parish for young adults. According to Charles Morris, who described St. Monica's in his book, *American Catholic*, the Sunday evening Mass there "looked like a *Baywatch* convention, packed with more than a thousand almost uniformly blond and tanned young adult singles and couples."[14] People come to St. Monica's from all over the west side of Los Angeles. The classic styling and beauty of the church and the impeccably maintained facilities make a wonderful first impression on the visitor. A comprehensive website links the parish to the broader community.

St. Agatha's is a poor parish in South Central Los Angeles with mostly Hispanic and African American parishioners, though it also draws a diverse group from the Los Angeles area. Two of its six weekend Masses are celebrated in Spanish. There are sixteen-hundred households or members registered. It is listed in Paul Wilkes's book, *Excellent Catholic Parishes*.[15]

---

13. I would like to acknowledge the work of three of my graduate students who assembled the data on these parishes, Brian Conroy, Jo Newville, and Leslie Jenal.

14. Charles R. Morris, *American Catholic: The Saints and Sinners Who Built America's Most Powerful Church* (New York: Random House, 1997), 299.

15. Paul Wilkes, *Excellent Catholic Parishes* (New York: Paulist Press, 2001), 200.

Dolores Mission, in the middle of the Pico-Aliso housing projects in East Los Angeles, the largest housing project in the western
United States, is a Hispanic parish with many undocumented immigrants. As the parish is unable to keep a register, the number of families is not available. One member of the parish staff described the
everyday experience of the parishioners as "crime, potential and
actual violence, serious poverty, government relief, immigration,
police and city agencies, unemployment, etc."

In the efforts to describe the evangelical effectiveness of these
parish communities, I will draw on two sources. First, Thomas
Sweetser offers a list of eleven indicators in his book, *Successful
Parishes: How They Meet the Challenge of Change*.[16] Second, keeping in mind Peter Henriot's critique of the 1988 study of liturgical
renewal in fifteen U.S parishes,[17] I would like to suggest that a good,
evangelical liturgy should result in a higher level of social concern
and service. Building on these works, I'd like to suggest the following
six criteria for our review: vital liturgy, shared ministry, adult faith
development, RCIA/full communion programs, community outreach, and welcoming the marginal. We will look at our three
parishes in light of these criteria.

1. *Vital Liturgy.* Father Sweetser observes that for most parishioners, "the Mass will be their only contact with the parish or the
Church."[18] Therefore, the quality of the liturgy is of first importance.
Is it alive, involving the assembly, giving expression to a diversity of
roles? Does it help foster a sense of community, and, at the same time,
maintain a sense for the transcendent? Does the music energize the

---

16. Thomas P. Sweetser, *Successful Parishes: How They Meet the Challenge of
Change* (Minneapolis, Minn.: Winston Press, 1983), 187–201.

17. See Peter J. Henriot, "Liturgy and Social Concerns," in *The Awakening
Church*, 117.

18. Sweetser, *Successful Parishes*, 188.

assembly and sustain a dialogue of ritual action, prayer, and song? Does the preaching enlighten minds and touch hearts?

It is universally agreed that what draws people to St. Monica's is its liturgy. Some years ago the parish brought in consultants to assist in the development of its liturgical program. Today the parish has a vital, "pumped up" liturgy; people drive from all over Los Angeles to participate. My reporter described it as "well planned, professional, enthusiastic, and polished." Though there is a full complement of lay liturgical ministers, both men and women, the priest is no adjunct minister; he presides and preaches. All services are supported by cantors and/or choirs, and even Sunday celebrations of baptism have lectors and ushers. The professional quality of the music "approaches the threshold of entertainment," but contributes to a liturgy that remains authentically prayerful. Because of parking and seating limitations, people begin gathering forty-five minutes before the popular Sunday evening liturgy.

Liturgy at St. Agatha's usually takes at least an hour and a half. Welcome signs and ministers abound. The buzz is deafening as people greet each other as friends. Before the opening procession, a lay minister leads the congregation in invoking the Holy Spirit on the assembly. The opening procession involves not just presider and liturgical ministers, but all present members of the pastoral council, accompanied by a rousing hymn and the "church mother" in the front pew shouting "alleluia." The robed gospel choir is racially mixed. Homilies generally go about half an hour—powerful preaching, but very informal, often addressing by name various members of the congregation present. When the liturgy goes longer, the creed and some sung Mass parts are skipped. No one leaves early and people are expected to stay afterward for coffee and conversation. One question: Does the exuberant liturgy leave any space for quiet and contemplation?

Liturgies at Dolores Mission are mostly in Spanish, standing room only, with one Mass in English. Though not up to standards of contemporary liturgists, the worship of the community and the strong influence of liberation theology themes clearly drive its many involvements. Music is simple but strong, with lyrics projected on an old movie screen. An emphasis on praxis is evident in the preaching. Only part of the assembly receives communion; the heart of Dolores Mission is its call to empowerment in response to the community's daily experience of poverty and injustice.

2. *Shared Ministry.* Is the parish run from the top down by the pastor or by a small parish staff, or is there a diversity of ministries that support its life? How are important decisions made? How many full-time and part-time ministers and how many programs and organizations does the parish have? Do parish ministers, ordained and nonordained, have a sense for enabling the ministries of others in the community?

St. Monica's has a parish staff of twenty full-time paid lay ministers, including two pastoral associates who are women. Clergy include a ubiquitous pastor, an associate pastor, and two priests in residence. Charles Morris says that its pastor, Monsignor Lloyd Torgerson, is probably the best preacher he encountered in the considerable visiting of parishes across the country he did for his book, while the quality liturgy he provides is in harmony with the great medieval liturgical tradition.[19]

St. Agatha's has a dynamic pastor, a lay pastoral associate, a permanent deacon, business manager, a director of teaching ministry, confirmation coordinator, coordinator of the *Apostolado Hispano*, maintenance manager, administrative secretary, teaching and Hispanic ministry assistant, music minister, nurse, and a summer day camp director. The style of leadership for what is considered the parish family is "collaborative." The pastor meets monthly with the pastoral council, a group that represents the many different communities, interests, and cultures of the larger parish. Standing committees are

---

19. Morris, *American Catholic,* 299–300.

responsible for individual spiritual formation, community building, and outreach. No major decisions are reached without the consent of the entire parish.

Dolores Mission's ministry has four Jesuit priests on staff, an administrator, school principal, religious education director, coordinator for the base communities, youth director, and an executive director of *Proyecto Pastoral.* The ministry of the parish is shared through the fifteen or more base communities that the parish hosts.

3. *Adult Faith Development.* Do members of the congregation gather to share their faith, take part in scripture study groups or adult education programs? Are they moving toward an adult understanding of their faith and a mature spirituality? Are they taking an active part in the life and direction of the parish?

St. Monica's sponsors an incredible variety of programs on prayer, spirituality, and adult education, using some of the best speakers in the archdiocese. Most of these take place on Sundays, as many people commute great distances and could not be there during the week. Each month, courses are offered on topics such as Celtic spirituality, Jewish-Catholic dialogue, contemplative prayer, and Christian meditation. For returning Catholics, a course called Checking out the Church is regularly scheduled over a six-week cycle.

St. Agatha's has numerous faith development and catechetical programs. Four times each month there are preparation programs for infant baptism, in Spanish and in English. Couples planning to be married must meet with the pastor six months before the celebration. On Saturday mornings, there are programs for 300 junior high and high school students in the public schools as well as family catechesis classes in Spanish for their parents, with 50 to 75 attending each Saturday. *Quinceañeras*, a Mexican tradition for the coming of age of fifteen-year-old girls, are celebrated as an opportunity to evangelize them. Confirmation classes are held twice a month; high school students and adults must attend. Special programs for the Spanish-speaking include: Mary's Angels, a program for young girls focused on human and Christian formation; marriage encounter; a Thursday evening Bible study; young adult group; charismatic prayer group; and several small faith community groups for evangelization, scripture, and faith sharing.

4. *RCIA/Full Communion Programs.* The parish RCIA program can be a very effective indicator of a parish's evangelical vitality. How many are preparing for baptism or for reception into the church? And is the RCIA program supported by the prayers and interest of the parish members?

St. Monica's has 80 to 90 candidates for baptism and reception into the church each year; at the Easter Vigil for 2001, over 120 were baptized or received into the church. One staff member described the parish as a "welcome back church." Each week, the parish staffs a Welcome Table for visitors and newcomers to the parish who meet staff members and learn about the various programs available. Those who leave their names and phone numbers are called *within the week.* The daughter of the graduate student who did the survey was so impressed with her visit that she signed up herself. The Welcome Table is set up even after baptisms. Because of this program, the parish recently registered its 2000th new household. The parish also has an evangelization coordinator who has a master plan for evangelization designed by a parish committee.

St. Agatha's had 17 candidates this year—3 adults (English speaking) and 14 children who are catechumens, all of whom are bilingual.

Dolores Mission does not have an RCIA program because no one comes for it. Most living within the parish boundaries are nominal Catholics. Evangelization means trying to reach the unchurched at significant moments for individuals or families (*quinceañeras*, first communions, funerals, and so on) and encouraging them to become involved in the community. Here again, in a congregation for whom liturgical participation is more occasional than regular, the liturgy plays a key role in evangelization.

5. *Community Outreach.* What programs does the parish have for the poor and the disadvantaged, particularly those in the local community? Does it cooperate with and share programs with other churches and organizations in the neighborhood? Is it active in the ecumenical and interreligious efforts of the diocese?

Santa Monica is an upscale community, but with its balmy climate it has a very large homeless population. The graduate student who visited there said that he had heard stories of "life enriching experiences" with the homeless the community seeks to serve. With such a large group, St. Monica's has joined a consortium with other churches in the community. The pastor works with three other parishes to serve the disadvantaged. According to the archdiocesan report, "Together in Mission," St. Monica's has the highest level of giving for the archdiocesan annual campaign. Its published goal is based on a percentage of the total parish income during the previous year.

With its central city location, St. Agatha's sponsors numerous outreach ministries. To keep children away from the often violent streets, the parish runs a summer day camp from the end of June to the end of August. Accredited by the American Camping Association, it offers a full program, including a Wednesday field trip for children from kindergarten through eighth grade. Older children participate as junior counselors or counselors-in-training. The cost is $125 per week, with financial assistance for families who cannot afford it. The *Clinica* QueensCare offers basic medical care for a $5 donation, which includes pap smears and breast exams for women as well as prostate exams for men. There is a tutoring ministry on Tuesday evenings and Saturdays to help elementary and high school students with their homework. The community assists the St. Peter Claver Center with a monthly food drive, a special Thanksgiving collection, and a Christmas Adopt-a-Family program. S.H.A.R.E. (St. Agatha Hands Are Reaching Everywhere) provides an annual Christmas dinner for the homeless, as well as gifts, services, and companionship.

Community outreach for Dolores Mission is focused through two groups. Community in Action (CEA) is the community's grass-roots organizing arm and has succeeded in a number of initiatives: increasing the police presence at the Pico-Aliso housing projects by over one-hundred officers, closing alleys, having speed bumps installed to deter drive-by shootings, and having storm drains and sewers cleaned. It also holds information sessions on welfare and immigrant rights. Liturgy at Dolores Mission does not take place only in church. The parish organizes *caminatas* or peace marches after acts of violence, gang shootings, or to raise consciousness on immigrant or housing issues. There are about thirty of these *caminatas* a year, plus one every Friday night to make three of the Stations of the Cross on the streets of the neighborhood.

Another very successful ministry is the Guadalupe Homeless Project (GHP), which helps the largely male immigrants who come to Los Angeles without jobs, providing temporary shelter in the church building at night and showers. The women of the parish take turns providing hot meals. The GHP also helps immigrants find long-term housing, provides access to medical service job referrals, and information on workers' rights, legal aid and referral, weekly classes in English, and classes on the prevention of venereal disease.

There is also a very significant outreach to young people from the parish, many of whom are involved in gangs. The emphasis is on prayerful reflection on their experience, using the Sunday readings and meditations written by Michael Kennedy, S.J., Dolores Mission's pastor.[20]

6. *Welcoming the Marginal.* In all parish communities there are many who do not "fit in," among them youth, single adults, the divorced, shut-ins, inactive Catholics, gays and lesbians, immigrants, the poor. Do people from these groups find a welcome?

---

20. See Michael Kennedy, *Eyes on Jesus* (New York: Crossroad, 1999), *Eyes on the Cross* (New York: Crossroad, 2001), and with Michael Sheen (narrator), *The Jesus Meditations: A Guide for Contemplation* (New York: Crossroad, 2002).

Are there specific programs to meet their needs? How are visitors welcomed and invited to become involved? Is there an outreach to inactive Catholics in the community? Sweetser asks: "Can people have a loose association with the parish and still feel they belong there?"[21]

The members of the pastoral team at St. Monica's place a high priority on meeting people's needs; this is their pastoral vision. Those needs are very different. Half of the congregation is on the liberal side, half very conservative. The young people in the parish tend to be politically conservative, but are more progressive on church issues. They want to see conditions change, and often become more progressive on social issues as they become involved in parish activities. A priest on staff described St. Monica's as having a "hidden diversity consisting of separated, divorced, homosexual, and other categories of people who don't feel particularly welcome in their home parish." One lesbian couple reported that they were turned away by four other parishes before St. Monica's welcomed their child for baptism. It is one parish where openly paired gay couples can be seen. The parish directory lists roughly forty widely diverse ministries and projects. They have a Bible study, a charismatic prayer group, and the Legion of Mary as well as a ministry for divorced and separated Catholics, a young ministering adults group, a gay and lesbian outreach, an AIDS ministry, an older adults ministry, in addition to the usual liturgical, music, religious education, and retreat ministries.

St. Agatha's is a richly diverse community, with many mixed-race families and children. The gay and lesbian community is welcome. It has a bereavement ministry for families that have experienced the loss of a loved one and another to bring the Eucharist to the sick and homebound. The golden-agers provides opportunities for seniors to take a more active life in the community.

---

21. Sweetser, *Successful Parishes*, 196.

The Dolores Mission Alternative School serves fifty or more marginal students, among them teenage mothers or gang members on probation. The Jobs for a Future, directed by Father Greg Boyle, S.J., helps gang members or other young people "at risk" by providing job training and placement, as well as operating a number of businesses: Homeboy Bakery, Homeboy Silk-screening, Homeboy Production Cleaning Services (for movie sets), and Homeboy *Artesiana*. It also offers free tattoo removal in conjunction with a local hospital. The Dolores Mission Women's Cooperative Child Care Center offers day care as well as classes for adults in early childhood education for certification, college-level English, ESL, and mathematics. *Imaginando Mañana* (Imagining Tomorrow) offers a variety of programs aimed at preventing violence among the four gangs battling for turf in the neighborhood.

Conclusion

A concern about lackluster liturgies and ineffective preaching should not blind us to the many successful parishes across the country, as Paul Wilkes illustrates in his book.[22] Furthermore, it's important to keep in mind Father Sweetser's comment, mentioned earlier, about Sunday Mass being the only contact with the church for many Catholics. Since far too few Catholics subscribe to Catholic magazines or journals, the Sunday liturgy represents a unique opportunity for evangelization and education in the faith.

The communities we have considered here represent the rich diversity of Los Angeles. Two of them experience daily the poverty, violence, and crime of their inner-city neighborhoods. But in each, a care for both liturgy and preaching has played a major role in

---

22. Paul Wilkes, *Excellent Catholic Parishes*.

developing them as vital communities of faith, worship, and service. They are, to paraphrase Pope John Paul II, living ecclesial communities, sustained by an intense liturgical life. They are indeed successful instruments for evangelization. Perhaps we won't have to go to the tent.

Chapter 5

Evangelization as Conceptual Framework for the Church's Mission: The Case of U.S. Hispanics

Allan Figueroa Deck, S.J.

The terrorist attacks have the potential
to shake us out of our individualism,
hedonism and consumerism....Historically,
U.S. Catholics have not had a major impact on
U.S. culture, and many have succumbed to its
negative consumerism, opening up a chasm
between their faith and their American
culture....The immigration that flows
from culturally Catholic areas such as
Latin America also has the potential for
increasing the church's influence on
American culture....

Cardinal Avery Dulles, S.J.[1]

1. Reported in *America*, December 3, 2001, 5.

Allan Figueroa Deck, S.J.

Throughout his 1999 post-Synodal Apostolic Exhortation, *Ecclesia in America,* Pope John Paul II proposes evangelization as the conceptual framework for understanding the church's fundamental task in both North and South America.[2] While there are many differences rooted in history and culture between North and South, the "new evangelization" proposed by the pope requires one to view the church's ministry in these lands integrally and in terms of solidarity. There are too many connections, interdependencies, interrelated challenges, and possibilities for the local churches to continue viewing themselves in isolation. In this document, therefore, the pope chooses to use the word *America* in the singular to refer to what we often call "the Americas" in the plural.

Something analogous can be said about the evangelization of U.S. Hispanics. Sooner, rather than later, it is necessary to conceive of this process in connection with the larger one, namely, the evangelization of U.S. culture *across the board.* For many reasons, it is normal in both social and religious circles to isolate Hispanic questions, to sharply distinguish them from some normative "mainstream." The central issues that frequently concern church leaders, the media, and even academics pertain to a mainstream to which the Hispanics by definition do not belong.

This way of thinking fails on several counts. The demographic changes are dramatic indeed. For example, the majority of U.S. Roman Catholic children ages 1 to 9 are of Hispanic origin. In the key states of California, Texas, Florida, New Jersey, New York, and Illinois, Hispanics are already either the majority of Roman Catholics or are well on their way to becoming so.[3] If, indeed, youth is the future, then Hispanics are the future of U.S. Catholicism.[4]

---

2. *Ecclesia in America* (Washington, USCCB, 1999).

3. Dramatic demographic gains for Hispanics are verified in the U.S. Census for 2000.

4. The National Research and Resource Center, Instituto Fe y Vida: Stockton, Calif., December 2000.

Moreover, the growing interdependence and interaction of cultures with the larger society at social, economic, and political levels mean that issues of Hispanic ministry can no longer be neatly contained.

The prevailing attitude toward ministry in both Anglo American and Hispanic contexts often fails to view it properly as "a moving target" subject to many developments. It betrays a rather static way of thinking, one that reifies and regularly oversimplifies a complex reality, making the task of evangelization all the more difficult.

I. Toward an Integral Vision of Evangelization

The church's contemporary understanding of evangelization requires a dynamic, fluid vision of cultures. In this ongoing process one culture is not seen as somehow above another but rather all cultures, especially the hegemonic one, are seen through the lens of Christian faith.[5] The gospel of Jesus Christ, while influenced by many cultures, transcends them all. It is important also to add that the cultures in question include what is called the culture of modernity and postmodernity propagated as never before by globalization.[6] Modern culture goes beyond national or ethnic cultures. While its paradigmatic expression is American, it takes root in virtually all cultures through the powerful influences of mass media.[7]

The target of evangelization is precisely culture in all its manifestations. If one ignores, downplays, or fails to grasp what culture is

---

5. Pope Paul VI, *On Evangelization in the Modern World* (Washington, D.C.: USCCB, 1975), no. 20.

6. *Ecclesia in America*, no. 20.

7. Alfred C. Krass has taken the concept of evangelization as developed in Catholicism and merged it with his understanding of Protestant evangelism. He uses many Roman Catholic sources, including Pope Paul VI's *On Evangelization in the Modern World* in his *Evangelizing Neopagan North America* (Scottdale, Pennsylvania: Herald Press, 1982).

and how it works, especially its fluidity and pervasiveness, one can hardly evangelize.[8]

Americans have a particularly hard time in being reflective about their culture. One of its features is precisely an orientation toward action, not contemplation. The United States came about over against the "old world" and its cultural and religious divisions. Americans came to think of themselves as somehow beyond those things. Theories do not excite them. They are a "can-do" people looking to the future. Forget about the past—especially your native language and ethnic identity. Learn English, work hard, subscribe to the civic religion's democratic values, assimilate, and that is all. This formula has more or less worked. Today, however, many wonder what the price has been.

This mind-set, nevertheless, appears to be undergoing some modification as a result of events in the second half of the twentieth century: the human and civil rights movements, feminism, and the new migrations. The terrorist attacks of September 11, 2001, have also prompted reflection on values and possibly a reassessment of U.S. culture. These trends call into question the nature of the historic American assimilation process as ambiguous, the purveyor of both values and dis-values from the point of Christian and human values. The famous "cultural wars" of the 1990s manifest a reflectivity regarding culture new for the United States. Be that as it may, many Americans, among them many Catholics, are still uncomfortable with cultural analysis and critiques. As long as that is so, a deeper understanding and acceptance of evangelization in the U.S. Catholic Church will be difficult to achieve.[9]

Many years ago, I made this contention in *The Second Wave: Hispanic Ministry and the Evangelization of Cultures,* a textbook on

---

8. Pope Paul VI, *On Evangelization in the Modern World,* no. 17 and 18.

9. Avery Dulles addresses this issue directly in "Pope John Paul and the New Evangelization," *America,* 166 (February 1, 1992), 70.

pastoral ministry among U.S. Hispanics.[10] The book is still in print perhaps because in the intervening years, to my knowledge, no other book has appeared that addresses the pastoral reality of U.S. Hispanics in a somewhat systematic way with a clear methodology and ministerial vision. First of all, at the heart of the pastoral method used in that book is the simple but often neglected principle that in ministry and pastoral planning one must proceed inductively, not deductively. You must know the people and their reality first and, if at all possible, come to *love* them.[11] *Then*, one may proceed gingerly to evangelize, catechize, educate, and form the community. Second, the book's underlying ministerial vision is taken directly from the normative documents of the Roman Catholic Church's magisterium regarding its identity and mission as expressed in the rich and nuanced concept of evangelization. Yet, its meaning unfortunately remains quite illusive to many Catholic leaders.

A Well-Kept Secret

Many years after the Second Vatican Council and Pope Paul VI's landmark apostolic exhortation *On Evangelization in the Modern World,* vast sectors of ecclesial leadership have only a notional knowledge of what evangelization means *according to the magisterium.* There is plenty of rhetoric about evangelization in ecclesial circles. In the majority of cases, unfortunately, the word becomes a cliché and is emptied of its real content. Often, it means merely the fostering of some form of vigorous outreach like home visitations or ministers of hospitality at the parish. While these are praiseworthy steps in the long and arduous process of evangelization, they hardly get at its core meaning.

---

10. Allan Figueroa Deck, *The Second Wave: Hispanic Ministry and the Evangelization of Cultures* (New York: Paulist Press, 1989).

11. St. Augustine of Hippo made this point clear in his masterful treatise on religious education titled *De doctrina christiana,* book 4, chapter 12 in *The Fathers of the Church* (New York: The Fathers of the Church, Inc., 1950), vol. 2, 193.

Indeed, evangelization is the second well-kept secret of contemporary Catholicism—the first being Catholic social teaching! Actually, the church's stress on social justice and its option for the poor are integral dimensions of the evangelization process.[12] So, if evangelization is a well-kept secret, so is Catholic social teaching and vice-versa.

Liberal-Conservative Polarizations and Culture Wars

There is another reason why evangelization has not succeeded in capturing our attention. While the Second Vatican Council and the spirit of the past thirty-five years of church renewal were supposed to be *pastoral*, they have often in practice become *ideological*. Ideology is the enemy of pastoral praxis. This is so because individuals and groups become polarized over their pet notions of doctrine and bog down in a kind of arrogant rationality.[13] On the one hand the liberals were enthralled by the Second Vatican Council, and on the other some conservatives were alarmed. Strong pockets of conservative reaction arose shortly after the reforms of the Second Vatican Council began to take shape. The passion with which liberals, conservatives, or even centrists responded to issues such as the renewal of the liturgy, ordination of women, changing views on homosexuality, theological trends in ecclesiology and Christology—to name just a few—was often, in my view, an obstacle to being inductive about anything. One is wrapped up in arguments and pet theories, in apologetics new or old. One is at war, as it were, caught in a dialectical treadmill, reacting to something and hence not truly open.

---

12. See P. Surlis, "The Relation between Social Justice and Inculturation in the Papal Magisterium," in Ary Roest-Crollius, ed., *Creative Inculturation and the Unity of the Faith* (Rome: Gregorian University Press, 1986). Also see, *Ecclesia in America*, no. 58.

13. I develop this thought in some detail in Allan Figueroa Deck, "A Pox on Both Your Houses: A View of Catholic Liberal-Conservative Polarities from the Hispanic Margin," in Mary Jo Weaver and R. Scott Appleby, ed. *Being Right: American Catholic Conservatives* (Bloomington, Ind.: Indiana University Press, 1995), 88–104.

The Catholic Pastoral Imagination Eclipsed

One way to speak about what has happened is to refer to David Tracy's idea about the Catholic analogical imagination, the Catholic sensibility that allows believers to hold in tension apparent contradictions and inconsistencies. Rooted in Mediterranean cultures, the Catholic analogical imagination thrives on ambiguity. This imagination allows for more tolerance of diversity and flexibility in the interpretation of rules than the more rigid approach of Nordic Protestant cultures in which modernity took root early in the sixteenth century. This Catholic sensibility came under siege by modernity's tendency toward literality and univocal thinking. Andrew Greeley also relates this trend to the Protestant,[14] dialectical imagination with its drive toward clarity and consistency. The modern world's drive toward literacy, clear and distinct ideas, and its ability to get propositional knowledge out there through print makes us all—whether liberals or conservatives—captives of a subtle form of the dialectical imagination. Hispanic cultures, in contrast to the highly literate cultures of Europe and the United States, continue to be residually oral as Walter J. Ong, S.J., has pointed out. In oral cultures, authority is in persons rather than in propositions or abstractions. Rules are thus subject to more personal interpretation than in literate cultures where things are "spelled out in black and white."[15]

The Lack of an Evangelizing Pastoral Theology

The drive for clarity short-circuits the contemplative stage. One does not look simply at what is with expectation or detachment, much less expect to be surprised. Yet that is what a pastoral vision

---

14. Andrew Greeley, *The Catholic Myth* (New York: Charles Scribner's Sons, 1990), 147–49.

15. Walter J. Ong, *The Presence of the Word* (New York: Simon and Schuster, 1967), 111–20.

91

rooted on the idea of evangelization requires. Fidelity to the core beliefs and practices that establish and nourish Catholic identity is one thing; a hard-crusted dogmatism of either right or left is another.

The terrible truth is that one may appear to be right theologically and be wrong pastorally. You may be working out of sound doctrine and ideas, but are translating these truths with dialectical passion into the pastoral reality without adequate reflection or adaptation. It is generally accepted that "all theology is ultimately pastoral," yet much of it is done with little or no reference to context and matters of practicality. One must contemplate the reality and come to know and love the context and the particular people being served. Christian praxis informed by a theological vision is all about leading others to the truth in love. In my years of pastoral ministry, the impression I have is that the liberals fail in this regard as much as do the conservatives.[16] A pastoral approach, therefore, excessively driven by doctrines and not tempered by an in-depth experience of culture and openness to social, economic, and political contexts, is unlikely to promote evangelization as it is understood today by the church.

The Vatican II Generation: Passions and Discontents

My generation of U.S. Catholic Church leaders is among the most passionate promoters of the Second Vatican Council. We *knew* the pre-Vatican II church and understood all too well the reasons for the *aggiornamento*. Even though the meteoric rise of the church's self-understanding in terms of evangelization is due to the Second Vatican Council, the word *evangelization* itself is, nevertheless, problematic and bothersome to many of the otherwise pro-Vatican II generation of baby boomers. The term is identified with proselytism, something diametrically opposed to the spirit of Vatican II with its

16. Cardinal Dulles describes the difficulty some theologians have had in doing theology in a way that relates effectively with the church's mission to evangelize. See Avery Dulles, "Evangelizing Theology," *First Things*, 61 (March 1996).

teaching on religious liberty and appeal for dialogue and church unity. That is why one will hardly hear the word *evangelization* on the lips of many U.S. Catholic leaders, including clergy and bishops, many years after *On Evangelization in the Modern World*.[17]

An interesting illustration of this came in the form of an anecdote told to me about the experience of a U.S. Jesuit at an international meeting of the Society of Jesus in Rome. He informed Jesuits in attendance from other nations that the use of the word *evangelization* is not acceptable to many in the United States because it is identified with proselytism, and that the good Fathers and Brothers might consider using another word. There was not time to explain to him that what is meant today by *evangelization* is not proselytism. The international Jesuits simply had to inform him that in today's global church evangelization expresses the underlying vision and identity of the church. Evangelization of cultures provides the *conceptual framework* for what the church, and one might hope, the Jesuits are all about!

In my own experience, not just in the U.S. Jesuit context, I have noted the different attitudes toward the notion of evangelization as I move from English-speaking to Spanish-speaking situations. In the latter, the language of evangelization is much more acceptable. For all these reasons, then, it appears that U.S. Catholicism is seriously out of phase with worldwide Catholicism on how it has received the church's teaching on evangelization. Evangelization is the tune that the church plays today as it marches on in mission. Yet, if I am correct, that tune remains faint background music in the United States.

---

17. The CARA Catholic Poll identified four generations, each with a different attitude toward the Second Vatican Council: the pre-Vatican II Generation, the Vatican II Generation, the post-Vatican II Generation, and the Youth Generation. CARA reports on these differences and describes the main features of each generation. See *The CARA Report*, 6/4 (Spring 2001).

Allan Figueroa Deck, S.J.

Evangelization in a Nutshell

The bibliography on church teaching regarding evangelization is immense. For me, the basic sources for a well-rounded understanding of evangelization are the Second Vatican Council's *Gaudium et spes* (1965), especially number 56 and following, Pope Paul VI's *On Evangelization in the Modern World* (1975), and Pope John Paul II's *Ecclesia in America* (1999). In these documents of the magisterium, evangelization is defined as a process of ongoing conversion by which the gospel of Jesus Christ is proclaimed. The process of evangelization stands on three legs: inculturation, liberation, and ecumenical and interreligious dialogue.

First, the conversion process begins with the human heart but includes one's family and community. The target or object of the church's evangelizing activity is not just individuals but most especially those often illusive collectivities called culture: a people's values and their way of feeling, thinking, and acting. *Inculturation* is the encounter of the gospel with culture and their mutual penetration.

Second, the conversion process necessarily affects the social, economic, and political order. The central gospel command regarding love of God and neighbor requires attention to results in the real order of things. The central teaching of Jesus Christ, the reign of God, is about love manifesting itself concretely now and into the future. Transformative social action flows naturally from a heart centered on Jesus Christ and his reign of justice, love, and peace. Catholic social teaching is about this constitutive element of evangelization: *liberation* from sin and all its concrete, personal, structural, and systemic effects.[18] Consequently, evangelization as liberation is about transforming the social, political, and economic

---

18. There is a strong link between the concept of evangelization and Catholic social teaching that lays out the implications of evangelization as liberation. See Pope John Paul II's discussion of "structural sin" in *On Social Concern (Sollicitudo rei socialis)*, no. 37 (Washington: USCCB, 1988).

order. Yes, it is about politics understood as matters of public, local, national, and international policy, not partisan party politics.

Third, *ecumenical and interreligious dialogue* is a fundamental dimension of evangelization because the gospel is about God's universal love and the presence of God's spirit in all persons, not just in the Catholic Church but in other Christian churches and in non-Christians as well. The concept of dialogue is not just a matter of method. Dialogue refers to an attitude of mutuality, respect, and solidarity rooted in human dignity. It is a requirement of love as incarnated by Jesus Christ himself. He exemplified it in his teachings, especially the parables that challenged their hearers to "think outside the box." Jesus' gospel message invites its hearers to reflect on their attitudes toward themselves and others, especially the poor and marginal in their midst, in ways that frequently go beyond the received prevailing truths of one's social class, culture, and religion. While Catholics believe that all the truth necessary for salvation is found in the church, they also affirm that truth, important truths, about God and human reality, life here and life beyond, can be found in the searching, practices, and beliefs of those who do not even know Jesus Christ. For this reason, the dialogue required by evangelization is always characterized by true *mutuality*.[19] To proclaim the gospel is to promote the ongoing search for the truth in love, not to merely sit on the important truths one has received, no matter how sublime, or mindlessly repeat them.

The New Evangelization

In the 1990s Pope John Paul II added a substantial element to the church's understanding of evangelization. He coined the phrase

---

19. In addition to the sources already cited in this section, the documents of Vatican II that support this vision of evangelization are *Gaudium et spes*, especially no. 56 and following; the Decree on Missions, *Ad gentes*, no. 22; the Decree on Ecumenism, *Unitatis redintegratio*, especially no. 2; and the Declaration on Religious Liberty, *Dignitatis humanae*, nos. 9–12.

"the new evangelization" and defined it as "proclaiming the gospel with new methods, expressions and ardor."[20] He and the bishops gathered at various regional synods have noted the contrast between commitment to and enthusiasm for mission among Catholics and among Evangelical Christians. The new evangelization is a call to intensify the church's efforts at reaching out to others, whether they be alienated from the faith of their ancestors or have never or hardly heard about Jesus Christ. The notable success of Evangelicals, especially Pentecostals, in attracting people, particularly the poor, to their Christian communities provides some lessons that the church must heed. Evangelization accordingly is linked to the church's ancient call to mission and apostolicity.[21]

Mainline churches like the Roman Catholic are perceived to be somewhat moribund in the United States, to be satisfied with maintaining institutions and structures but not moving on from there. They seem to lack inspiration. The new evangelization is a reminder of the need not only for sound ideas and concepts in pursuing the church's mission but of *esprit* or what in Spanish is called *mística*. It is not only a matter of knowing and loving the cultures to be evangelized as well as the social context, of having a good theology, pastoral method, and planning, but of *spirituality*: personal and communal prayer, faith-sharing, and the affectivity of devotion or zeal.

---

20. Pope John Paul II first used this definition of the new evangelization in his address to the bishops of CELAM on March 9, 1983. He reiterates it in the opening address at the Fourth General Conference of the Latin American Episcopate on October 12, 1992, in Santo Domingo. This address is available in a translation by Phillip Berryman in Alfred T. Hennelly, ed., *Santo Domingo and Beyond* (Maryknoll, N.Y.: Orbis, 1993), no. 10, p. 47.

21. Pope John Paul II outlines the major features of the new evangelization in *Ecclesia in America*, nos. 66–74.

II. Critical Issues in the Evangelization of U.S. Hispanics

The first part of this chapter was an attempt to present the background for understanding what evangelization means as the fundamental conceptual framework the church offers us today as we go about pursuing our very identity and mission as Christians. Now, I will turn specifically to U.S. Hispanics with a view toward identifying six critical issues that arise in their evangelization.

1. Leadership and Lay Ecclesial Ministries

Leadership at every level, that of the ordained clergy as well as that of the laity, is a basic requirement for the evangelization of U.S. Hispanics. As Abraham Lincoln reminded us: "Where there is no vision, the people perish." Leadership has to do primarily with communicating a compelling and appealing vision. Evangelization as outlined in the church's documents and in the ministry of Pope John Paul II *is* the vision that the church proposes today. However, there appears to be a lag between that vision and its timely communication at all levels of the community.

The Latin American bishops were truly the first regional grouping of bishops to take the Second Vatican Council's and subsequent articulations of evangelization seriously. The Medellín Conference in 1968 offered a striking vision of evangelization in the particular context of Latin America. It was followed by the Puebla Conference in 1979. Latin American liberation theology was a laudable if flawed effort to take evangelization as inculturation and liberation seriously.[22]

---

22. Two useful assessments of the accomplishments and limitations of the age of liberation theology in Latin America are José Comblin, *Called for Freedom: The Changing Context of Liberation Theology* (Maryknoll, N.Y.: Orbis, 1998); and Guillermo Cook, ed., *New Face of the Church in Latin America* (Maryknoll, N.Y.: Orbis, 1994).

U.S. Hispanic bishops were familiar with the work of their Latin American colleagues. They began to articulate this vision for U.S. Hispanics in several documents as well as in the *encuentro* processes of the 1970s and 1980s. The National Pastoral Plan for Hispanic Ministry provides a vision grounded on evangelization that is still a worthwhile outline of the implications of this integral vision.

The U.S. Bishops' Committee on Hispanic Affairs recently issued new directives called *A Pastoral Framework to Further Develop Hispanic Ministry*.[23] Certainly it can be said that at the level of documentation the foundations for an evangelizing vision have been laid. Unfortunately, it is articulated in isolation from the greater whole that is the broader U.S. church. This is understandable because the overarching vision provided by evangelization is still not the preferred framework within which the U.S. Catholic Church as a whole and its leaders view themselves. But this must change.

One might ask why to this very day there has not been any visioning and planning process comparable to the *encuentros* for the *entire* U.S. church. Hispanics were allowed their *encuentros*, but the wider church was not. The normal mechanisms by which bishops, pastors, priests, deacons, religious, teachers, and catechists communicate a vision to their local churches have not yet succeeded in presenting the issue of evangelization with the cogency and urgency it requires. For whatever reasons, those involved in the formation of leaders in seminaries, theological and diocesan centers, and Catholic universities have ignored or simply prescinded from the idea of evangelization. Consequently, there are bits and pieces of the vision out there but little integration of it.

Pope John Paul II put it this way: "The renewal of the Church in America will not be possible without the active presence of laity. *Therefore, they are largely responsible for the future of the Church.*"[24]

---

23. Reported in *The Tidings*, Archdiocese of Los Angeles (December 7, 2001), 9.
24. Pope John Paul II, *Ecclesia in America*, no. 44 (emphasis mine).

What is the thrust of this "renewing action" of the laity if not evangelization, inculturation, liberation, and ecumenical and interreligious dialogue? This lay activity has certainly gone beyond the "pray, pay, and obey" of pre-Vatican II times, but it still may be circumscribed by a fragmented vision of church and an inadequate theology of ministry.

The failure to reach out and serve Hispanics to the extent required by their overwhelming numbers is due in great part to the inadequacy of the church's current ministerial structures. The church will never evangelize cultures at depth, to the core, without adequate cohorts of ministers that must sooner or later come from the cultural group itself. The system of ordained clergy and vowed religious that has developed over the centuries, especially since the reform of the Council of Trent, appears to me to be seriously compromised if not exhausted. What I mean is that current ministerial structures simply do not produce ecclesial leadership in the numbers and variety necessary to realistically deal with the challenges and opportunities in today's world. There must be an opening up of categories whereby married men and women, single laity, and youth are engaged more closely in as many forms of service in the church as they can while respecting what is truly proper to the ordained clergy and vowed religious. Otherwise the church cannot, will not evangelize. It is that simple. This does not mean that I expect the priesthood or the religious life to disappear. Rather, I expect them to be *reconfigured* in light of a renewed understanding of the common baptismal vocation of all.

Often the institutional logic of parishes, schools, and other Catholic organizations leads in the convenient direction of maintenance and self-promotion rather than the challenging one of evangelization—mission along the lines of spiritual conversion, social transformation, and ecumenical and interreligious dialogue.

Both Hispanics and the larger U.S. Catholic Church leadership need to get excited about this vision of evangelization. A business-as-usual mentality is precisely one of the factors holding parishes, dioceses, schools, and other Catholic institutions from reaching out to others and eventually integrating them into the larger community. For too many, this is a threatening rather than an exciting task. Yet that is what evangelization entails.

Leadership training for Hispanics grounded on the church's vision of evangelization is a vital need among Hispanics. That kind of training includes ecclesial lay ministries but must stress first of all the role of laity in transforming the world of family, work, and the professions. Too much effort is placed on ministries *ad intra* and, as a result, the evangelizing task is unwittingly truncated.[25] The primary role of laity is expressed precisely in taking the gospel down into every corner of human endeavor, making the gospel culture by enshrining it in the values, attitudes, and actions of one's society.

Much of the church's efforts are focused on maintaining its current commitments. An evangelizing church must willy-nilly review its financial commitments with a view toward fostering the kind of leadership needed by an evangelizing church. While the formation of ordained ministers and religious men and women has an important role to play in church leadership development, one may ask whether the distribution of church resources reflects an evangelizing vision. If it did, it would place more emphasis on the formation of laity. It is said that the lion's share of ecclesial resources, including finances, is committed to the formation of priests and religious rather than the formation of laity. Such a policy runs counter to the vision of church as evangelizing *in its entirety.*

This seriously affects the evangelization of U.S. Hispanics. Education and formation of every kind are urgent needs if Hispanics are to assume the roles of leadership that logically they must in the church and society today and tomorrow. While the percentage of

25. See Allan Figueroa Deck, "Latino Leaders for Church and Society: Critical Issues," in Peter Casarella and Raúl Gómez, *El Cuerpo de Cristo: The Hispanic Presence in the U.S. Catholic Church* (New York: Crossroad, 1998).

Hispanics involved in lay ecclesial formation programs has grown over the years, it is nowhere near the level that the demographics would suggest. Moreover, lay leadership formation programs of any kind are hard to find. Those that do exist sometimes fail to integrate a vision of evangelization into their curriculum.

2. The People's Religion

While progress has been made over the last twenty years in correcting the excessive enlightenment mentality in many pastoral agents, it is still an issue. Some of the training received in diocesan centers, seminaries, Catholic universities, and theologates was inappropriate for Hispanic ministry. Instead of disposing priests, religious, and lay leaders to relate with love and sympathy to the religious orientation of Hispanics, it gave them many reasons to be uncomfortable and suspicious of it. Latino theologians have done a good job of explaining the serious lack of pastoral sensitivity of mainstream church leaders to the religion of the Hispanic people. This is a fundamental issue that impedes evangelization.[26] The people's religion is a synthesis of their culture. If one rejects their popular religion, one rejects *them*. That, indeed, is what unwittingly has been going on in many a parish where there is simply little tolerance for the people's Catholicism.

What is necessary is a clearer understanding of the process by which popular religious rituals, symbols, and narratives can be *transformed*, not rejected. This requires going in the door of the Hispanic communities, with their exuberant, rich, and diverse customs and beliefs. The evangelization of Hispanic cultures began long ago with the first preaching of those late medieval Spanish Franciscan friars. A profound orientation to divinity and the world of the spirit began

---

26. Among the excellent treatments of popular religion by U.S. Hispanic theologians are Orlando O. Espín, *The Faith of the People* (Maryknoll, N.Y.: Orbis, 1997); and Roberto S. Goizueta, *Caminemos con Jesús: Toward a Hispanic/Latino Theology of Accompaniment* (Maryknoll, N.Y.: Orbis, 1995).

centuries before that in the complex and deeply spiritual world of their pre-Columbian ancestors. The process was enriched again by the vivid, visceral faith of African slaves. Now, in the United States, this popular Catholicism undergoes yet another inculturation.

3. The Ambiguity of Multiculturalism

The church's understanding of evangelization of cultures provides some serious correctives to the prevailing attitude toward multiculturalism in the United States today. Sociologist of religion John A. Coleman, S.J., points out many of the flaws in thinking about the issue of multiculturalism in both church and society.[27] He begins by stating: "Some appeals to multiculturalism are merely sentimental inclusive rhetorics which, in fact, do not honor cultural difference." He repeats the observation made by Robert Schreiter to the effect that migrations are creating multicultural societies for which there are usually no clear plans or policies regarding how such diverse peoples might live together. Documents of the magisterium have hardly ever used the word multiculturalism. Rather, pastoral and missiological practice going back centuries insists on the need to respect each and every culture and honor the people's particular language.[28] The process of evangelization presupposes a safe, homogeneous environment that will render a people open to the challenges of the gospel. The truths and values of that gospel will most adequately be communicated in the mother tongue with metaphors, allusions, and gestures that speak to the heart of a people.

The incredible diversity of Catholic ethnic groups and cultures in the U.S. church today represents an enormous challenge. I have

---

27. John A. Coleman, "Pastoral Strategies for Multicultural Parishes," *Origins* 31/30 (2002), 497–505.

28. See Allan Figueroa Deck, "Multiculturalism as an Ideology," in Allan Figueroa Deck, Yolanda Tarango, and Timothy M. Matovina, eds., *Perspectivas: Hispanic Ministry* (Kansas City: Sheed and Ward, 1995).

criticized the movement away from national or "personal" parishes as the new code of canon law refers to them and the trend that puts ever-larger, multicultural megaparishes in their place. While there can be no single formula for how to respond to such an enormous challenge, it is clear that from the point of view of evangelization there is need for a small community dynamic.[29] This creates the conditions necessary for a cultural group to negotiate its wider unity in the church through a healthy sense of its own security, dignity, and particularity. The dynamic of the large, often anonymous parish simply short-circuits this process.[30] In the conference mentioned above, Coleman outlines a strategy for multicultural parishes that takes the demands of an evangelizing church quite seriously. I will mention a few of the points he makes: (1) When immigrant groups are allowed to gather together in their own church environments their religious commitments get stronger; when merged too quickly with other groups they diminish. (2) A successful immigrant parish serves not only as a place of prayer but also as a community center where material, health, and social needs are often addressed. (3) Prayer and worship should not normally be multicultural; rather it should reflect the particular language and cultural and religious sensibilities of the people. Certainly, there are special occasions when the liturgy should reflect the entire diversity of the community. But those occasions should be relatively rare. (4) If space is to be shared with another cultural group, a decision must be made about how the

---

29. One of the leading writers on inculturation, Marcello Azevedo, maintains that a community context is the most propitious for evangelizing culture. He links evangelization with small Christian community dynamics in *Basic Ecclesial Communities in Brazil: A New Way of Being Church* (Washington, D.C.: Georgetown University Press, 1987).

30. The late Joseph Fitzpatrick, one of the leading sociologists of Hispanic religion in the United States, alludes to the serious concern regarding the abandonment of smaller, homogeneous parishes as a matter of policy in the second half of the twentieth century in "A Survey of Literature on Hispanic Ministry," in *Strangers and Aliens No Longer* (Washington, D.C.: USCCB, 1993), 63–87.

space will truly become that of both groups, that is, how will it be permanently designed and decorated. A sense of being on one's own turf is essential to creating the goodwill necessary for serious evangelization of cultures. (5) There must be a vigorous emphasis on leadership training. This will create the possibility of truly attending to the people with formed ministers who speak their language and love the culture, the sine qua non of effective evangelization.

4. The Challenge of Other Religions

The flight of Hispanic Catholics from the Catholic Church in both Latin America and the United States is a fact that has been repeated over and over again by the media. Elsewhere, I tried to outline the causes and possible responses to this very significant phenomenon.[31] Much light is shed upon this phenomenon by the church's understanding of evangelization. The movement of Latin Americans to Evangelical churches occurs because those churches are ministerially structured in such a way as to provide people with conversion experiences. The ritual, sacramental orientation of Catholicism with the woefully inadequate ratio of priest/minister to faithful does not adequately provide for the *personal attention* required by the conversion process that is basic to evangelization. For lack of ministers, the gospel message is often not communicated or heard in the traditional Catholic context. An evangelizing church, in contrast, has a sufficient number of ministers reaching out with the Word to others. This is the first but necessary step in the long process of conversion.

---

31. Allan Figueroa Deck, "The Challenge of Evangelical/ Pentecostal Christianity to Hispanic Catholicism," in Allan Figueroa Deck and Jay P. Dolan, ed., *Hispanic Catholic Culture in the United States* (Notre Dame, Ind.: University of Notre Dame Press, 1994), 409–39. Also see M. D. Litonjua's most perceptive overview of this issue in "Pentecostalism in Latin America: Scrutinizing a Sign of the Times," *Journal of Hispanic/Latino Theology*, 7/4 (May 2000), 26–49.

Hispanic Catholics often sense that they have not taken personal responsibility for their faith. They have been exposed to the *indirect* experience of God through mediations such as the sacraments and sacramentals, saints, the church itself, the priest, and so forth. Yet, they have seldom been told about the possibility of the *direct* experience of God. In the context of modernity and postmodernity, Hispanics yearn for opportunities to have a free, personal encounter with the living God. Unless the people are lucky enough to experience a *cursillo* or a charismatic prayer group, a *kairos* or search, they may never develop a more self-appropriated faith. In a word, they will remain only partially evangelized!

Pope John Paul II's emphasis on the new evangelization and the need for communicating the faith with more *ardor* relates quite directly to the methods and expressions used by Evangelicals and Pentecostals. There is a level of sustained affectivity in this form of Christianity that for various reasons may sometimes be lacking in Catholicism. For one thing, the faith became routine over the centuries; for another, the rationalism of the clergy, teachers, and theologians in the Catholic Church tilted the presentation of doctrine in the direction of conversational tone, catechetical formulas, or even academic discourse. What the ordinary people are looking for is the preaching of the Word with conviction and power, with "fire in the belly."

In the United States, moreover, the middle-class status of the majority of Catholics creates situations in the local parishes where the Hispanic people who are in the majority working class feel uncomfortable. Community is difficult to bring about in the context of social class and cultural difference. The policy of placing Hispanics in middle-class, multicultural parishes, while well-intentioned, does not help create the best conditions for evangelization. A small, relatively *homogeneous* community is, all things being equal, a better context for evangelization. It renders people open and benevolent, while the impersonality, anonymity, and growing diversity of the large suburban parish generally does not. The Evangelical churches offer Hispanics exactly that: small, relatively homogeneous community, strong affectivity, and ministers formed to receive and communicate in the people's own language, with their gestures and root metaphors.

Yet, it must be said that the approach of Evangelical churches certainly does not conform to the full concept of evangelization as understood in the Catholic Church. There is usually little emphasis on liberation and there is even less on ecumenical or interreligious dialogue.[32] With regard to inculturation, however—engaging the gospel with the people's culture—Evangelical churches often do very well indeed.

5. Evangelization as Liberation

The religion of the poor is often seen as an alienating, superstitious affair that holds the people back from serious engagement in the public square. Matters of social, economic, or political import are simply bracketed from their religious life. The church's vision of evangelization, however, insists that faith and justice go together. As a result, the hidden sources of motivation and meaning in the people's faith that empower them to act must be made explicit. This is precisely what happened in the most successful social movement in the history of U.S. Hispanics, the United Farm Workers Union led by César E. Chávez. The hidden power of the Guadalupan symbol was evoked in such a way as to galvanize the community for the

---

32. Ralph C. Wood, a Baylor University professor and committed Evangelical, provides a critique of his own co-religionists. I paraphrase his letter to the editor in which he laments some possible negatives in contemporary evangelicalism: "...Our revivalism leaves converts cut off from the church; our decisionism rests on sub-Christian notions of autonomy; our pietism robs us of reverent worship; our devotion lobotomizes the life of the mind; our clean living gives us contempt for those who smoke and drink; our biblicism makes us ignorant of the bi-millennial Christian tradition; our exclusivism convinces us that Roman Catholics are not Christians...." See *First Things*, 119 (January 2002), 8–9.

social struggle experienced now as an integral dimension of their Catholic faith and Mexican culture.

The key religious symbols of Latin American Catholicism— Mary, the suffering Christ, and saints like Martín de Porres—can all be interpreted in the key of social, economic, and political justice. Mary is no longer the suffering, silent woman, but rather the author of the Magnificat who boldly talks about "putting the mighty down from their thrones." Christ suffers as he identifies himself with every oppressed person who ever was or will be. His suffering is redemptive; it brings salvation, liberation, and healing. Through it we can be healed not only in spirit but also materially, socially, economically, and politically. Saints like Martín de Porres, Juan Diego, or Rosa de Lima can be understood as examples of God's loving presence in the lives of the poor, marginal, and forgotten of this world. This hermeneutic of liberation is not merely an arbitrary "spin" put on these traditional symbols. In fidelity to the message of Christ and to the church's most authentic traditions, these symbols and the function they play in the church's mission to evangelize are understood precisely in the key of faith and justice.[33]

6. Upward Mobility and Evangelization

David Hayes-Bautista and Mario Barrera have raised a critical issue. Are Hispanics choosing the road of *assimilation* and simply blending into the secularized Protestant cultural ethos of the United States? Or are they opting for *integration*, that is, finding creative ways to engage their U.S. cultural context without losing all their *hispanidad* and Hispanic Catholic ethos? The answer is

---

33. Christopher Tirres and Allan Figueroa Deck, "Latino Popular Religion and the Struggle for Justice," and James W. Skillen, "Evangelical Cooperation in the Cause of Racial Justice," in Gary Orfield and Holly J. Lebowitz, eds., *Religion, Race and Justice in a Changing America* (New York: The Century Foundation, 1999), 137–52 and 115–36, respectively.

not yet available.[34] But the issue relates quite directly to the goal of evangelization. Some of the Hispanic values, especially its family and commmunity orientation, are central Christian values. Some of the U.S. values are also central Christian values: human rights, personal dignity, and the drive toward equality. How can these two gospel orientations be reconciled in such a way that Hispanics will make a true contribution to the evangelization of American society? This is the point made by Cardinal Dulles in the quotation with which we started. A place to begin is with a more perceptive understanding of cultural transformation. Cultural literacy is a fundamental requirement of an engaged, intelligent Christian today. This will provide tools for *cultural discernment.* Since culture is usually taken for granted and most people are quite unconscious about how it really influences them, there is an urgent need for knowledge regarding how culture really works. The church's understanding of evangelization of cultures (inculturation) flows directly from insight into this anthropological concept of culture as "the air we breath, the way we express our humanity."

Hispanics today do experience upward mobility as a result of education and economic advancement. There is a growing Hispanic middle class. What does this mean in terms of cultural values? Will Hispanics settle for the individualism, hedonism, and consumerism noted by Cardinal Dulles? Or will Hispanics constitute a new, even improved form of American citizens? How will intermarriage influence all those "mainstream" non-Hispanics and their children who may be exposed to Hispanic values? To the extent that this question becomes more urgent, will there be a growing possibility of true evangelization of U.S. culture? Otherwise, cultural changes will be governed by the powerful subliminal messages of advertising and the

---

34. See David Hayes-Bautista, "Mexicans in Southern California," in *The California-Mexico Connection*, Abraham F. Lowenthal and Katrina Burgess, eds. (Palo Alto, Calif.: Stanford University Press, 1993), 146. Also see Mario Barrera, *Beyond Aztlán* (Notre Dame, Ind.: University of Notre Dame Press, 1988), 63.

media and by the logic of the marketplace, and not by the more humane values of U.S. or Hispanic cultures or by the gospel of Jesus Christ.

Conclusion

The church's understanding of evangelization provides a cogent, well-wrought framework for pastoral leaders in the United States. Given the dramatic rise of Hispanics in U.S. culture, especially in the church, an urgent, central concern regarding that vision hinges on the need to confront both U.S. and Hispanic cultures with the gospel of Jesus Christ. This dual action requires a deep love for and a critical sense of *both* cultures. A clear gospel-based critique of Hispanic cultures is needed, one that does not play into the anti-Hispanicism of the Black Legend[35] or other prejudices. It will take a close look at how *machismo* and some other features of Hispanic cultures work against human dignity, especially that of women. This critique will also look closely at the negatives of individualism, hedonism, and consumerism in U.S. culture.

This vision also requires Catholic leaders to integrate the church's social teaching into every aspect of life. This social or prophetic orientation finds its source in the life of prayer and intimacy with God and others in community, especially in the Eucharist and in Christian spirituality. In addition, evangelization requires that ecumenical and interreligious dialogue become a way of life for Catholic Christians in an increasingly pluralistic world.

To adopt the church's understanding of evangelization as *the* framework for today's and tomorrow's mission is a challenge that requires serious rethinking of curricula in catechesis, religious formation, and Catholic education for priests, religious, and laity across the board. This rethinking ought to affect theology, preaching, and

---

35. A prejudice against Spanish culture developed by the enemies of Spain.

teaching at every level of the church. It must inspire the lives of laity in business, labor, academia, the media, arts, education, and the professions. The response so far to Pope John Paul II's call for a new evangelization has been lackluster in my view, especially in the United States. Yet the church's future vitality depends upon a renewed commitment to this magnificent vision, one of the principle legacies of the Second Vatican Council and still a most urgent task.

Chapter 6

What Catholics and Evangelicals Might Learn from Each Other about Evangelization

William R. Burrows

What follows is mainly reflection on my experience with Protestant Evangelicals in collaborative work with them as an editor in a Catholic book publishing house, and as a theologian with a special interest in mission and evangelization. One of the most satisfying areas of my career in the past few years has come through working with men and women belonging to the so-called Evangelical movement. Some are card-carrying members of the Evangelical Theological Society, but most are in three mission studies groups—the Gospel in Our Culture Network, the American Society of Missiology, and the International Association of Mission Studies. Some of my colleagues, I should add, are wary of formal identification with the label *Evangelical* for various reasons.

111

A Key Point of Contact for Catholics and Evangelicals

As we enter the twenty-first century, a great divide exists within churches. My interpretation of it and problems that attend the question of evangelization in contemporary North America, I hope, will cast light on why a large group of Center-Right Catholics and Center-Left Evangelicals find friendship with each other stimulating. In it they seek to address the gospel message to a North America that is at once religious, religiously diverse, and fearful of being forced into "totalizing" systems.[1]

In my experience, how one defines the task of "gospeling" or "evangelization" in relation to the following two questions reveals the polarities: Is the Christian vocation to evangelization best expressed as the ministry of preparing people to accept Christ into their individual lives, as they align themselves with God's goal of reconciling all humanity and the universe in the way that texts such as Romans 8:18–25 (on the cosmic scope of redemption) suggest? Or does using the language of Paul enshrine the neo-Platonic vision of heaven-earth separation that liberal theology showed was a bad interpretation of Aramaic and Hebrew cosmology? The implication, of course, is that such concepts alienate Christians from the mission to alleviate human suffering now, as one sees prescribed in synoptic gospel texts such as Luke 4:18–19 (on proclaiming the release of captives and letting the oppressed go free).

No one with knowledge of the subject matter answers a simple yes or no to such questions. Nevertheless, the people I am calling

---

1. For an overview of the general religious situation and an account of its continuities and discontinuities with North American religious tradition, see Andrew Greeley, "Religion Is Not Dying Out Around the World," *Origins* 23 (June 10, 1993), 49–58; Wade Clark Roof, *Spiritual Marketplace: Baby Boomers and the Remaking of American Religion* (Princeton: Princeton University Press, 1999); Wade Clark Roof, *A Generation of Seekers: The Spiritual Journeys of the Baby Boom Generation* (San Francisco: HarperSanFrancisco, 1993); and Tex Sample, *Ministry in an Oral Culture: Living with Will Rogers, Uncle Remus, & Minnie Pearl* (Louisville: Westminster, 1994).

Evangelicals tend to put more eggs in the explanation basket that goes with a yes answer to the first question. I dislike the use of the term *liberal* or *liberationist* to delineate those who put more eggs in the second basket. Using liberal to differentiate Evangelicals from those whom they judge reduces the gospel to its this-worldly social dimensions, but, nevertheless, is common. Reluctantly, I follow the convention, even though I know the word is too crude to identify the nuances in each position.

Overall, then, I suggest that American Catholics suspicious of key aspects of the liberal or progressive wing of post-Vatican II Catholicism find conversation with American Evangelicals to be productive and full of insights. Both they and classic Protestant Evangelicals take their cues on evangelization from the Gospel of Paul. They accentuate the entrée into Christianity as one of entering personally into a relationship with Jesus and his followers in the Spirit. Classical Evangelicals affirm the literal teaching of scripture to be the test of authenticity, and are experts at identifying those who waver. Neo-Evangelical Catholics start to get nervous at just this point. They fear being forced into a box that keeps out the wisdom of tradition, the "sense of the faithful," and a poetic-mystical sensibility for the ironies of God's ways of self-revelation.

In all cases, the critical moment in becoming Christian, according to the Evangelical, is the conscious acceptance of Christ, and inviting him into one's heart. Drawing attention to the need for conscious acceptance of Christ and at least the theoretical subordination of every other aspect of church life to that conscious decision, is the Evangelical movement's greatest gift to American Catholics. As a church that practices infant baptism, Catholicism has long relied on the natural process of birth and family habits of belonging for its new members. As a church with two thousand years of tradition, even Vatican II's calls to reform can appear burdened with Byzantine complexity. Catholicism's reverence for propagating itself through natural birth and its complex structures lead to its major pastoral problem. How does the church bring "nominal" Catholics and the fallen away into conscious, committed membership?

Most cradle Catholics, including myself, bridle at the language of being reborn, even when we know its biblical sources (John 3:3–8). It is not our kind of language. Nevertheless, for many Catholics, beginning to understand the Evangelical emphasis on conscious rebirth through full acceptance of Christ has become the entrée into an appreciation of Evangelicalism itself. The insight into what Evangelicals mean by it and the way in which it cuts through layers of cultural accretion in Catholicism stems at least in part from Evangelicalism being de facto the prototypical American form of Christianity.

At the same time, Catholics tend to be suspicious of Evangelical litmus tests rigidly applied. The prototypical form of Christianity most Catholics imbibe with their mother's milk is akin to a hermeneutic preunderstanding of church as a big tent. Fervor and commitment among its members are desirable, but we presume that they will differ immensely, and there is no great emphasis put upon any individual to adopt the Johannine gospel language of rebirth. Instead, despite the renewal of sacramental theology since Vatican Council II, the pastoral principle for Catholics largely remains that of the Council of Trent: The sacraments convey grace "to those who do not put an obstacle in their way."[2]

To Evangelicals, that practice carries with it the danger that we underestimate the existential nature of the decision for Christ and overestimate the instrumental role of the church and its sacraments. In addition, the question posed to Catholics by Evangelicals in an age when society's structures do little to support faith is: Will the communities that undergirded the sense that God could be met in a deeper dimension of everyday life celebrated in the sacraments long survive?

These are more than contemporary versions of classical Reformation objections to Catholicism. To make my personal biases

---

2. Council of Trent, Canons on the Sacraments in General, canon 6.

concrete, I realized in the late 1980s that I am at least a fellow traveler with Evangelicals. With them I believe that evangelization (viewed from the side of the evangelizing agent) is foremost a process of inviting people to allow God into their lives at a deeply personal level. In saying yes to the person of Christ, one is saying yes to God. Evangelicals mediate that commitment with the Word. Catholics certainly try to use the Word, but it is my sense that the church and the sacraments become a mediating system that softens the decisiveness of the commitment, a decisiveness that Evangelicals put front and center with rituals such as the "altar call."

I do not mean to deprecate the richness of the sacramental tradition. When one realizes that what it is supposed to mediate is an encounter with God, in turn mediated by Christ, one knows also what Edward Schillebeeckx means when he says that the sacraments are sacraments of encounter with Christ, who is himself the primal "Sacrament of God."[3]

Having come to that conclusion, I found that I was having some of my most energizing and interesting conversations with Evangelicals. At one level, each of us retained fundamental disagreements, particularly in matters of ecclesial versus biblical authority, but at another we found ourselves appreciating each other's insights into the nature of being Christian and the vocation of evangelization.

Sources of Catholic-Evangelical Resonance: Faith as Total Immersion in the Living God

To explain this dynamic, I find myself returning to 1969 and my first semester in Rome at the Gregorian University. When I have discussed insights gained from those days with Evangelicals, particularly

---

3. Edward Schillebeeckx, *Christ the Sacrament of the Encounter with God* (New York: Sheed and Ward, 1963), 133–40.

what I learned from the lectures on the theological virtues (faith, hope, and love) given by the Spanish Jesuit Juan Alfaro, I have found these insights to resonate with their ideas on the structure of Christian life. Alfaro's course was partly a retrieval of the doctrine of Thomas Aquinas, but it was rich also in reference to biblical and patristic sources, as well as to Luther and the Reformers.

Faith, Alfaro insisted, is not only believing in God and in certain things as revealed by God (*credere Deum se revelantem*, "to believe God revealing Godself"). Alfaro insisted that faith is also *cognoscere Deum* ("to know God [existentially]"). Though we begin to know God dimly and though our knowledge of God is dominated by anthropomorphizing images, in faith, according to Aquinas, we begin a process of knowing God personally in ways that no words could capture. Faith is an entry into a relationship with God mediated by the historical Jesus and the Holy Spirit.[4] As Alfaro developed the dynamics of faith, it involved also *credere in Deum*, which he termed a "movement toward salvation begun inchoately in justification and consummated in the vision of God [eschatologically]."[5]

The way of evangelization, if this be the case, is one in which the human being undergoes a radical reorientation of life by becoming Christian. Alfaro developed these themes with copious references to Patristic and medieval theology. For Alfaro, the author of books on Christian anthropology and the relationship between Christian hope and human liberation,[6] a prime task of theology in the post-Vatican II era was to integrate the transcendent dimensions of evangelization with the immanent ones of liberation.

---

4. See Juan Alfaro, *Fides, Spes, Caritas: Adnotationes in Tractatum de Virtutibus Theologicis* (Rome: Gregorian University Press, 9th ed., 1968), 7–15, 234–80.

5. Ibid., 197.

6. See Juan Alfaro, *Speranza Christiana e Liberazione dell'Uomo* (Brescia: Queriniana, 1971) and *Cristologia e Anthropologia* (Assisi: Citadella, 1973).

What has struck me with greater clarity ever since being introduced to the task of promoting human liberation by Alfaro in 1969 was the immense gulf between him and theologians who took their primary cues on the nature of theology from Kant, the Enlightenment, and contemporary cosmology. Alfaro moved to liberation from oppression as an integral goal of Christianity, to be sure. But the foundation of the move was the renewal of the inner person through dialogue with God. Because God was love, the closer the follower of Jesus began to realize his or her own nature, the more urgently the judgment that suffering needed to be alleviated and humankind freed from oppression would well up from within the disciple's breast.

The preoccupation of the Catholic magisterium since the early nineteenth century—when viewed charitably—there are other less charitable interpretations—has been to combat the reduction of Christianity to what moderns will accept, on the one hand, and, on the other hand, to overcome the subjectivism and skepticism that critical thought since Kant has brought into theology. In exactly this context, Catholics and Evangelicals in agreement about the evangelization of the contemporary world are also joined in the task of articulating a faith that refuses to be reduced. It is a faith that believes the Christian worldview to be better grounded in reality than modernity, for the Christian worldview is founded on the "knowledge" that God, transcendence, and the holy can break through the limits of history and relativity, and that in faith we can know God.

In Alfaro's construal of the Christian habit of mind and heart, "faith" (*fides quae creditur*, "faith as that which is believed") is the community's possession. Theology is *sapientia* ("wisdom") that guides one on the path to total immersion in the life of God. Evangelization is the beginning of a gospeling process in which the Spirit leads the individual to feel the pulse of God (*fides qua creditur*, "the faith by which it [faith] is believed"). In other words, the internal testimony of the Spirit mediates the presence of the living God and leads one to entrust oneself to Christ in faith.

Entering this zone of faith, one discovers that Christic life includes all of life. Such things as good and evil, justice and injustice, friendship and indifference, self-transcendence and self-absorption, love and hate, creativity and entropy, life and death are where the Christian experiences life "Christomorphically." That is to say, in Schleiermacher's account of it, "Christ exercises a forming, re-forming, informing influence upon the matter of human nature and human religion."[7]

Theological Orientations and the Goals of the Gospeling Process

Theology seeks to work out the relationship between what the Christian as an individual and the church as the community of faithful know in faith, and what they know through life in the worlds of science, art, politics, and culture that Christians share with every human being. While everyday theological discourse is directed to helping Christians understand what they believe and how faith should direct them in practical affairs, apologetic theology tries to make the case for both insiders and outsiders that Christian wisdom and knowledge are not irrational. Indeed, that the leap of faith enables one to see reality with a deeper reason. Suffice it to say here that the Christian who believes Christ is the light of the world (John 8:12) needs to be able to give reasons for hope in the truth of this claim (1 Pet 3:15).

At stake is the tradition's understanding of itself and the world. Theology at the service of evangelization needs to show why the leap

---

7. I take the term "Christomorphic" (Christ plus the Greek morph, "form,") from H. Richard Niebuhr, *Schleiermacher on Christ and Religion* (New York: Scribner's, 1964), 212.

of faith Christians make (on the basis of the external testimony of scripture and tradition and the internal testimony of the Holy Spirit) discloses horizons of meaning more adequate than its competitors. While such apologetics is not fully "objective," it can at least explain why the community judges that Christianity should be chosen over its competitors.

Evangelization, I am trying to say, is aimed at helping the convert share the mind and heart of Christ and see the world with new eyes. It is not merely giving the prospective convert a few lessons in the history of Israel and Jesus, in addition to some facts on how the church carries on his mission. There is much to be said for honest research into the Jesus of history, the Christ of faith, and the problems of reconciling them. Indeed, faith is no substitute for letting historians do their work honestly. But an evangelical theology is constructed on the notion that there is something of an entirely different order present in Jesus than a wise man. Yet much of modern theology is built on reductionism. It discounts the testimony of a great cloud of witnesses that Jesus as the Christ is uniquely human and divine, decisive for the salvation of the world, the one in whom God is not only revealed but who is himself God. The church's tradition has it that when one responds to the person of Christ, who beckons us to walk with him in the Christic Way, something radical occurs under the power of the Holy Spirit.

The Evangelicals with whom I share and from whom I gain light on the evangelizing mission of the church have a live sense that mature Christian identity is an affair of the heart. They see Christian life as often being a struggle with a God who sometimes demands superhuman effort. They believe that evangelization is the process of introducing a person to the struggle to open one's self to God in the Spirit of Christ. That struggle is a microcosm of the universe's struggle to find fullness in God.

In all this, I have been moving toward saying that what draws a certain kind of Evangelical and a certain kind of Catholic together is the sense that they have a common goal in gospeling contemporary North America: to manifest holistically the Christian way of meeting God as the clue to knowing oneself, to living life in its fullness, and to participating consciously in reality's destiny. Evangelicals and Catholics are drawn together by a sense that from each other they will learn better how God's self-revelation is the way to become fully human. Yet, precisely here lies a problem for Christian communities with a deep sense of identity. They easily become self-satisfied, arrogant, self-righteous, and insular. If we are not clear about the depths and power of secularity's critiques, Catholic and Evangelical convergence on what the gospeling process entails will go nowhere.

In the struggle to respond to modernity's criticisms, in the words of Bernard Lonergan, "the defenders [of faith] were left in the unenviable position of always arriving on the scene a little breathlessly and a little late."[8] Rather than meet those criticisms convincingly on its own grounds, the papacy tried to keep a lid on modernism within Catholicism, sometimes at a great cost to Catholics who were forced to stifle their intellectual lives to remain in good graces with the church. At the Second Vatican Council (1962–1965), the gates to modernity were opened and since 1962 Catholics have plunged into the fray, trying to make out the difference between proper *aggiornamento* ("updating") and capitulation to secular modernity. In the eyes of Pope John Paul's Curia, much post-Vatican II modernization had come to be viewed in October of 2000 as a surrender to relativism.[9]

---

8. Bernard J. F. Lonergan, *Insight: A Study of Human Understanding* (New York: Philosophical Library, 1958), 733.

9. Congregation for the Doctrine of the Faith, "Declaration *Dominus Iesus* on the Unicity and Salvific Universality of Jesus Christ and the Church," Rome, August 6, 2000. Cardinal Joseph Ratzinger signaled his concern with relativism earlier in an address to eighty bishops; see "Relativism: The Central Problem for Faith Today," *Origins* 26 (October 31, 1996), 310–17.

While much more could be discussed, the thing that must be said is what links this to our topic, evangelization. In my experience, the kind of Catholics and Evangelicals who are interested in talking together about the evangelization of North America tend also to view theological modernization as having achieved highly ambivalent results. Their concern crystallizes around agreement that the church should take its cues on the task of evangelization from the Gospel of Paul.[10] In both cases, though, the key act of the Christian is that of entrusting oneself to Jesus the Christ as teacher, savior, and healer.

What I am driving at is that the great divide within the Roman Catholic and the Protestant traditions is between those who are and those who are not persuaded that critical modern thought is the most reliable way of deriving religious and theological "truth."

Correlating Two Typologies of Evangelization

The Protestant Evangelical Model

Historically speaking, Protestant approaches to evangelization in the United States follow free association models. They are congenial to the American character's penchant for "voluntarism." If there is a need, people get together and try to meet it. If the means they adopt is successful, then people elsewhere notice and try to put it to work. In the ability to feel comfortable with ad hoc connections and networks, as opposed to formal ecclesiastical unions, lies the chief difference between Catholics and Evangelicals. It is also one of the areas in which each tradition has much to learn from the strengths of the other.

In a magnificent essay, Andrew Walls reminds us that—though much frowned on by European theological sophisticates (among

---

10. Compare similarities of emphasis in the Lausanne Covenant (1974) and Pope John Paul II's encyclical on mission, *Redemptoris missio* (1990). Point by point, they utilize the apostle Paul's writings as warrants for their positions.

whom I include Vatican curialists and popes who refer to such churches as "sects")—American "overseas missions were a continuation and extension of home missions."[11] First evangelization, Walls goes on to note,

> was the delivery of the elements of the Christian Gospel…couched in terms which sought individual commitment, while recognizing the family unit and creating and strengthening local *communitas*. This approach both channeled emotion and permitted the development of a popular culture; it also suggested a continuity with old traditions while being manifestly free of old institutions. This concern with primary evangelization differed from most European thinking of the same period. Contemporary Europeans were aware of a religious crisis, but they generally thought of it as a pastoral crisis. Their concerns were about building churches large enough and in the right places and getting the right sort of ministers to staff them, about the place of the church in a national system of education, and about preventing the state countenance of antichurch or anti-Christian influences.[12]

If one reads Pope John Paul II's *Ecclesia in America*, there is much to suggest that the pope has learned a great deal about the need to move from nominal membership in and support of institutional Catholicism and toward knowledge of and deep, personal commitment to Christ.[13] There is, though, no indication that he believes that

---

11. Andrew F. Walls, "The American Dimension of the Missionary Movement" in his *The Missionary Movement in Christian History: Studies in the Transmission of Faith* (Maryknoll, N.Y.: Orbis Books, 1996), 221–40, at 227.

12. Ibid., 228.

13. John Paul II, *Ecclesia in America* (January 22, 1999), a "post-Synodal apostolic exhortation…on the encounter with the living Jesus Christ: the way to conversion, communion, and solidarity in America."

Evangelical successes show that Catholics have anything serious to learn about changing the shape and organization of their church. Yet, in what Manuel Castells calls "the network society," Phillip Berryman suggests that Catholicism may be at a serious disadvantage in trying to carry out its evangelizing mission.[14]

Quoting Castells, Berryman notes that a network society involves a shift from vertically directed bureaucracies to the horizontal corporation (p. 23). Churches arranged horizontally, notes Berryman, are built around process, not task. They work by team management and the concept that a church ought to measure its evangelical performance by "customer satisfaction."

The Catholic Church, on the other hand, operates internationally on a model of "vertical bureaucracy." Priests and nuns, he notes, are lifetime employees and pastors are local branch managers. In the end, as in all bureaucracies, the "emphasis is on maintenance, not innovation" (p. 30). Berryman says that his proposal that Catholics consider use of the network model developed by Castells is "modest." It asks whether, in seeking to meet the religious needs of their members, mainline Protestant and Catholic churches "will, like large businesses, find themselves forced to adopt network styles—to reinvent themselves, to be re-engineered" (p. 33).

One must bear in mind that Berryman is thinking primarily of Latin America. Nevertheless, one of the things that North American Catholicism needs to take very seriously is the way in which Evangelicals are able to move into new areas and identify a need on the part of unchurched and nominally Christian people for a particular aspect of the gospel. Their relevance to the social situation of the people enables them to offer a message that brings such people to

---

14. See Phillip Berryman, "Churches as Winners and Losers in the Network Society," *Journal of Interamerican Studies and World Affairs* 41 (Winter 1999), 21–34. Samuel Ruiz García, *Mi Trabajo Pastoral en la Diócesis de San Cristóbal de las Casas: Principios Teológicos* (Mexico City: Ediciones Paulinas, 1999), 101–6.

Christ. They then form churches that nurture the convert and that quickly become self-ministering.

The Catholic Model of Evangelization

My broad-brush characterization of the Catholic approach to evangelization is that it is concerned mainly with regaining the allegiance of members who have fallen away from active church life. This is so whether the focus is on Europe, Latin America, or the United States. We seek to bring the lukewarm and fallen away back to the church, but the church to which they return is too often not one that can provide the kind of intimacy, nurture, and teaching that sustain faith.

I see few signs that the Catholic hierarchy believes that its church has much to learn from the horizontal networking methods of Evangelicals. In Pope John Paul II's apostolic exhortation *Ecclesia in America,* for instance, chapter 3, "The Path of Conversion," presumes that the Catholic Church, as presently organized, is the sole acceptable church in which to live out the teachings and desires of Jesus. As recently as March 2002, Cardinal Jorge Medina Estévez wrote to the bishop of San Cristóbal in the Mexican state of Chiapas, ordering him not to expand a system whereby four hundred deacons were serving as grass-roots pastors. The stated reason, according to the *New York Times* (March 12, 2002) is that allowing the Chiapas model to persist will send "a message of implicit support from the Holy See for an 'alternative' church model that could seem convenient for 'cultural situations and particular ethnic groups.'" In reading Bishop Samuel Ruiz's wonderful account of his pastoral planning, I see an incredibly sensitive pastor articulating a rationale for such "indigenous ministries" as a way to bring home to people the meaning of Christ. It seems such a pity that a man with an intimate acquaintance with the way Evangelicals and Pentecostals in Chiapas were showing how an evangelizing church could be constructed was first sacked and then had some of his most promising initiatives destroyed.

On a more positive note, *Ecclesia in America* also lays bare one of the riches that Catholic churches hold in seeing evangelization as a process ideally centered in liturgical life (virtually the whole of chapter 3). Catholicism's vision of worship as a key locus of evangelization is a manifestation of confidence in the power of the community's liturgical life to integrate the Christian mysteries and the rhythms of human life from birth through death. Indeed, the Catholic emphasis on transformation by participation in sacramental life has profoundly countercultural dimensions lacking in Protestant forms of worship that increasingly resemble modern forms of musical entertainment by pop stars.

Gathering Wisdom from Two Traditions

In the Protestant vision of evangelization, total intentional identification with the person of Jesus is the absolutely necessary condition for entrée into Christian life. This life is deepened by prayer and continuous Bible study that one shares with others struggling to become better Christians. In the Catholic vision, life in the church leads one deeper into life's meaning and finally to identification with Christ. In addition, because all of life, when properly understood, has a sacramental dimension, Catholic approaches to evangelization increasingly insist that gospeling in its fullest sense involves rooting out dehumanizing evil. For both Protestants and Catholics, liberation is integral to evangelization, because peoples oppressed by evil will be impeded from experiencing the fullness of their human dignity, nor will they grow into the fullness of life God wills for them in creation.

What is one to make of all this in contemporary North America? Let me begin with a cautionary note. First, we need to realize that the goal of evangelization touches the most private and highly disputed public dimensions of life. Second, because of the history of Christian missionaries intruding unasked and unwanted into the lives of non-Christians (both overseas and within North America), twenty-first century evangelizers must cultivate respect for the desires of those who wish to be left alone. I say this because I believe hard-sell preaching and evangelism-as-marketing are likely to corrupt an evangelization process in which the manifestation of Christ by authentic lives filled with love speaks louder than proclamation by words.

In that context, Pope Paul VI's apostolic exhortation *Evangelii nuntiandi* (1975) and the teachings of Pope John Paul II have a great deal of nuance and richness that Evangelicals may find salutary. I single out one of the most important when I observe that the Catholic position holds in tension two important truths. First, it does not water down biblical teaching on the significance and finality of Jesus as the Christ. Second, however, it recognizes that the case for Christ is often better revealed by holiness, love, and humility (*EN* 75), rather than by words.

Does this run the risk of not preaching the Word in the manner Paul models in 1 Corinthians 9:16, when he says: "Woe to me if I do not preach the Gospel"? I think not. Among other things, Paul was part of a tiny minority with neither power nor history. He was proclaiming something radically new in the midst of the *pax Romana*. The way in which Pope Paul VI envisages sharing the evangelizing word with a seeker made curious by the lives of loving followers of Christ seems to me far more culturally appropriate today. In North America, we are heirs to a European tradition that has lived with Christianity as a dominant religious tradition for up to fifteen hundred years. Our task is finding ways to help people who think they have good reasons for rejecting Christianity as bad news consider whether they need to take a second look.

First, evangelization is the beginning of a lifelong journey in Christian faith, love, and hope. In an age made cynical by the self-aggrandizement of television evangelists, by the predatory sexual behavior of some priests, and by advertising and propagandistic claim and counterclaim, a different way of inviting others to consider Christ needs to be found. That invitation, in the wisdom of the Catholic tradition of studying and emulating the lives of saints, entails being attracted to Christ, not being badgered into accepting him as savior in order to avoid hell. The wisdom of one of the foremost saints of our own day, Mother Teresa of Calcutta, is one of manifesting Christ more than verbally proclaiming him. Her path was one of learning to walk with Jesus, realizing in one's own life the Easter truth that life in its fullness comes through embracing death to self. One discovers that the Spirit of Jesus the Christ leads one deeper into the love of God, engendering hope that overcomes fear.

Catholics also have more than a little to learn from Evangelicals. I have already pointed out above in discussing the work of Phillip Berryman that associational models of networking at the grass roots may in many situations be more effective than trying to impose Catholic ecclesial structures. Those structures have developed since the fourth-century recognition of Christianity by Constantine. Since the twelfth century, they have included mandatory celibacy for presbyters. They are, in addition, resolutely patriarchal. In insisting that evangelization end in the implantation of the Roman Catholic system, instead of giving local Christians leeway to form fellowships and models for worship that suit their own cultures, the Catholic hierarchy, I fear, substitutes the *tradita* of tradition for traditioning, which is the soul of faith. Yes, Evangelicals might do well to realize the power of joining in sacramental enactments of the mystery of salvation and be more cautious about what often seems to be an overreliance on verbal formulas. Overall, my work with Evangelicals has convinced me that—if each church could learn to appreciate the wealth and authentic character of the apostolic tradition in the other—the way might be smoothed toward each tradition doing better in its evangelizing mission.

Evangelicals, in my experience, are at their magisterial best in pointing to the need to experience the dynamic of Christ's new life in the midst of life's problems. For Catholics, a host of rituals aims to bring one to the same experience. But Evangelicalism tries to guide the individual and the community to experience that truth consciously in the depth of the heart, and then to find in the scriptures the lens that helps them keep refining what conversion demands. In a North America where, increasingly, people are not buoyed up by extended families and communities, Evangelicalism's greatest weakness—its tendency toward individualism—is also its greatest strength. It is an approach to gospeling the lonely, anxious individual. Before Catholics bring out their standard critique of that individualism, I suggest that we need to recognize its strength. Deeply personal experience is not the enemy of the social gospel. Indeed, it may be the condition for implementing it and experiencing the truth of Romans 5:5. Paul says that the hope stirred up by hearing the gospel "does not disappoint because the love of God has been poured out into our hearts through the Holy Spirit that has been given to us."

Chapter 7

Evangelization in the Catholic Church: An Evangelical Reflection

Eddie Gibbs

Watching the Roman Catholic Church's response to the challenge to evangelize over the past thirty-five years has been a fascinating experience for this Evangelical observer. My first encounter was as an Anglican missionary in Chile in the latter half of the 1960s, when the documents of Vatican II had begun to be circulated. At that time I was part of an Anglican/Roman Catholic dialogue, which got some of us missionaries into hot water with our Evangelical Chilean friends; such were the tensions between the two communities at that time.

Then I remember the time I returned to Santiago, Chile, for a brief visit in 1974 when I sneaked into a training session for lay deacons taught by a leading Jesuit. President Allende had just been killed, with the military junta now in power seeking to use the Catholic Church as an ideological bulwark against Marxism. The event I attended felt like an Evangelical renewal meeting, with the evening concluding with a call to receive Christ in the heart and not simply in the mouth (a reference to the Eucharist). The atmosphere was electric, with one of the participants slamming his Bible shut and exclaiming, *"¡Que fantastico!"* There was hardly a dry eye in the room.

I also participated in some of the nationwide charismatic conferences and celebrations in the early 1970s, which brought Catholics and Protestants from a wide spectrum of traditions together in an atmosphere of rejoicing in the love of Christ for release and empowering of the Spirit.

Then, in the early 1980s, I met with priests of the Catholic Missionary Society in England to discuss the challenges they were facing in conducting parish missions aimed at reactivating lapsed Catholics. This is an urgent task for the Roman Catholic community in many parts of the world, especially in Latin America, where there is a strong motivation to reactivate dormant Catholics in order to safeguard them from the proselytizing activities of ardent Evangelicals and Pentecostals.

Since that time, it has been my privilege to engage in Roman Catholic and Evangelical dialogue within the archdiocese of Los Angeles. In that group, we have addressed many potentially divisive issues in a climate of trust and mutual appreciation. Those sessions spotlighted the common ground we share in the Gospel of our Lord Jesus Christ.

I begin my contribution with these vignettes in order to provide a context that has shaped my understanding of evangelization in the Catholic Church. Each of the incidents mentioned illustrates evangelization *within* the Roman Catholic community, as distinct from evangelization *by* the Roman Catholic Church, taking the gospel to those of other religious traditions and to the entirely secular. Also, I submit the following reflections as a personal response of someone who speaks from the Anglican tradition within the broader Evangelical spectrum.

The New Evangelization

I agree with the distinction drawn by Father Avery Dulles, S.J., in contrasting the positions of our two traditions, when he asks:

> Can the Roman Catholic Church be evangelical? Is Catholicism a religion centered in the Gospel? Half a century ago some Catholics, and practically all Evangelicals, would have said no. Protestant churches, it was thought, could be churches of proclamation and evangelization, but the Catholic Church was a church of liturgy and law, centered on tradition, hierarchy, and sacraments. In other words, Protestants were viewed as specializing in the word of God and the Gospel; Catholics, in the law of God and the sacraments.[1]

In the decades following Vatican II, there has been an increasing emphasis on the need to mobilize the Catholic Church for the twofold task of evangelizing its own and to take the Gospel of Jesus Christ to the ends of the earth. Only by mobilizing its total membership will the church of Jesus Christ be able to fulfill its great commission to take the gospel to all people in every generation.

In response to this challenge, both Paul VI and John Paul II established themselves as apostolic leaders. Their visionary leadership has outshone many Protestant or even Evangelical church leaders who have become bogged down in bureaucracy and internal agendas, such as top-down ecumenism, liturgical revision, women's ordination, and issues of human sexuality. Maintenance has displaced mission as their primary focus, in sharp contrast to the priority clearly articulated by Pope John Paul II in Mexico City on May 6, 1990:

---

1. Avery Dulles, "John Paul II and the New Evangelization—What Does It Mean?" in Ralph Martin and Peter Williamson, eds., *Pope John Paul II and the New Evangelization* (San Francisco: Ignatius Press, 1995), 25.

The Lord and master of history and of our destinies has wished my pontificate to be that of a *pilgrim Pope of evangelization,* walking down the roads of the world, bringing to all peoples the message of salvation.[2]

I remember the unprecedented visit of Pope John Paul II to Great Britain in 1982 when he spoke in a number of soccer stadiums to capacity crowds, with an impressive percentage of enthusiastic young people listening attentively. The pontiff's plain speaking, Jesus-centered messages issued a winsome challenge to take up the cross and follow Christ. An Anglican colleague, an ardent soccer fan, who later became a bishop in the Church of England, commented to me after watching the response of tens of thousands of young people in Britain to the pope's message: "I wonder how much his transfer fee is?"

Regrettably, John Paul II's laudable example did not always trickle down through the ranks of the parochial clergy or inspire the bulk of the laity. For only those who have experienced a real encounter with Christ are likely to be motivated to share that first-hand faith with others. At the same time that Catholic parishes were gaining new members through migration and a higher than average fertility rate among Catholic families, they were also losing significant numbers through the back door. In fact, as Avery Dulles admits, many were shifting their membership to evangelicalism "because Catholicism did not seem to offer them a real encounter with Christ."[3] *Evangelii nuntiandi* highlights the need for the church to be renewed by the Holy Spirit and in the discipling of its members. "Before the church can approach the word with credibility and divine unction it too must undergo a radical conversion, a profound change of mind and heart" (*EN* 10).

---

2. *L'Osservatore Romano* (English edition) (May 7, 1990), 1.

3. Dulles, "John Paul II," 37.

A further factor contributing to this hemorrhaging is the frustration of young people who find no real sense of community and little discipleship training, especially in huge parishes served by a single priest. Young people want to be involved through relationships in a trusting environment in which they can ask questions and explore the faith in an open spirit of inquiry. In this regard, both the Catholic and Protestant communities face a similar challenge, for both traditions are losing those under thirty-five at an alarming rate. The communication gap is exacerbated by the fact that 95 percent of the clergy are themselves on the wrong side of this significant age divide.

The need today is for the church not simply to be geared to the times but renewed in the power of Pentecost, for "the presentation of the Gospel message is not an optional contribution for the Church. It is a duty incumbent on her by the command of the Lord Jesus" (*EN* 5). Protestants in the Evangelical tradition readily identify with this insistence. The papal exhortation reflects true apostolic leadership in the sense of representing the apostolic drive of the early church to spread the good news. The pope's personal commitment to world evangelization issues a challenge to Evangelical leaders, because we have many Evangelical churches that do not engage in evangelization. John Stott, a leading Anglican scholar-pastor, admits as much in entitling a book he wrote on evangelization in 1967, *Our Guilty Silence*.[4] In many churches the great commission has become the "great omission"!

Agreement on the Central Truths of the Gospel

Mainstream Roman Catholic and Evangelical theologians share substantial agreement on the nature of the gospel.[5] Both

---

4. John R. W. Stott, *Our Guilty Silence: The Church, the Gospel and the World* (Grand Rapids, Mich.: Eerdmans, 1967).

5. See the report, *The Evangelical Roman Catholic Dialogue on Mission 1977–84*, edited by Basil Meeking and John Stott (Exeter, U.K.: Paternoster Press, 1984).

emphasize the reliability of the New Testament witness to the uniqueness of Christ, his virgin birth, his subsitutionary atonement on the cross, his physical resurrection, his personal return to complete his church, and the universal scope of his saving work. I am sure that Roman Catholics would have few problems with the definition of evangelism reflected in the Lausanne Covenant (1974).

> The Nature of Evangelism:
> To evangelize is to spread the Good News that Jesus Christ died for our sins and was raised from the dead according to the Scriptures, and that as the reigning Lord he now offers the forgiveness of sins and the liberating gift of the Spirit to all who repent and believe. Our Christian presence in the world is indispensable to evangelism, and so is that kind of dialogue whose purpose is to listen sensitively in order to understand. But evangelism itself is the proclamation of the historical, biblical Christ as Savior and Lord, with a view to persuading people to come to Him personally and so be reconciled to God. In issuing the Gospel invitation we have no liberty to conceal the cost of discipleship. Jesus still calls all who would follow him to deny themselves, take up their cross, and identify themselves with his new community. The results of evangelism include obedience to Christ, incorporation into his church and responsible service in the world (Paragraph 4).

The gospel consists of good news given by God the Father in the person of his Son and applied to the human heart by the working of the Holy Spirit. The grounding of this message is in the grace of God—that is his undeserved and amazing generosity toward sinners—which we could never deserve, and that is appropriated through faith. Gospel communication is essentially faith-based arising from the faith of the church in proclaiming the message, and in the faith of those who receive it. Herein lie some serious obstacles for the church. Those persons who have simply been socialized or sacramentalized without themselves being evangelized are unlikely to become bearers of the good news to others.

The Gospel and the Kingdom

In pre-Vatican II Catholicism there was a strong tendency to equate the institutional church with the kingdom. This is in contrast to dispensational evangelicalism that separated the present "church age" from the coming "kingdom age" representing the thousand years' reign of Christ on earth. However, this view was not generally accepted across the Protestant spectrum, and was more popular in North America than in Europe.

In both Catholic and Protestant circles during the past thirty years has come the realization that the gospel in the ministry of Jesus was *the gospel of the kingdom.* For Protestants, this meant the recognition that it embraced more than individual salvation, and for Catholics that the kingdom cannot be encapsulated in any institution. For both traditions, following the turbulent 1960s, the realization dawned that human effort cannot build the kingdom—whether that effort be represented by programs of evangelization or social service and justice, for ultimately, the kingdom is always a promise and a gift from God. It comes to us as God determines and often in surprising ways, from unexpected directions.

In both traditions, our understanding of salvation has been enriched and expanded as we have grasped the indissoluble link between *gospel* and *kingdom* and have explored the biblical dimensions of each of those complex terms. *Evangelii nuntiandi* makes a significant distinction and strikes a healthy balance between the spiritual and social dimensions of salvation. Salvation is indeed that "great gift of God which is liberation from everything that oppresses man but which is above all liberation from the Evil One (*EU* 9). This Apostolic Exhortation reflects the concern of church leaders and also of the Holy Father that the biblical concept of salvation not be subsumed under socio-political agenda to the extent that its core message of reconciliation with a Holy God through the atoning work of Christ is abandoned (*EN* 9). Evangelicals heartily endorse this concern. Although Evangelicals are still divided as to the extent to which evangelization includes social action, all would agree that the church

> reaffirms the primacy of the Kingdom by the proclamation of forms of human liberation; she even states that her contribution to liberation is incomplete if she neglects to proclaim salvation in Jesus Christ. (*EN* 34)

Eschatological Perspective of Evangelization

Recognition that the gospel is a message about God's coming kingdom and not simply restricted to individual salvation draws attention to the eschatological dimension of the message. The church is the community of God's people living God's future now, in an anticipatory sense. The kingdom was inaugurated with the coming of Jesus and will be consummated with his return. The renewal of humanity is not brought about by some utopian political program or revolution. The apostolic exhortation makes it clear that "there is no new humanity if there are not first of all new persons renewed by Baptism" (*EN* 18). In other words, there can be no kingly reign of Christ on earth without people who have submitted themselves to the rule of the king. Just as the old covenant embraced every area of life as itemized in the Torah, so the gospel of the kingdom addresses every area of life, personal and corporate. It is concerned with

> the rights and duties of every human being, about family life without which personal growth and development is

136

hardly possible, about life in society, about international life, peace, justice and development–a message especially energetic today about liberation (*EN* 29).

The Church as the Continuation of the Incarnation

This statement seeks to relate the ministries of the church throughout the ages to the continuing ministry of the ascended Lord. Even more, it expresses the mysterious nature of the church as the body of Christ. Christ and his church are inseparable. Not until his ascension could the church's ministry become his ministry. The church in turn is sent by Jesus to continue his work on Earth. For Jesus declared to his heavenly Father concerning his disciples: "As you have sent me into the world, so I have sent them into the world" (John 17:18). Then, in one of his post-resurrection appearances he commissioned his disciples, saying: "Peace be with you. As the Father has sent me, so I send you" (John 20:21).

Protestants have some reservations in describing the church as "the continuation of the incarnation," fearing that too close of an iden- tification will lead to the church replacing Christ, rather than witness- ing to him. Despite this concern, it is vital to reiterate the "profound link between Christ, the Church and evangelization." Within theology, there has been a tragic distancing between ecclesiology and missiology to the mutual impoverishment of each. Among Evangelicals who have had an ardent commitment to evangelization we have seen emerge a "churchless mission" through the activities of some parachurch agen- cies. There has been an attitude of mutual suspicion. On the other hand, we also have the specter of "missionless churches." From the standpoint of the New Testament, both terms are oxymorons.

One of the strengths of Catholic evangelism has been its ecclesial base and stress on community. This is in contrast to evangelization, as conducted by some Evangelical groups, which has been through "lone rangers" bringing individuals to "decide for Christ" without any linkup with a local church. The same problem emerges with big meetings held by itinerant evangelists. They face the chronic problem of how to link "inquirers" who respond to the evangelist's message with a participating local church. Evangelists of the stature of Billy Graham and Luis Palau make determined efforts to bridge the gap between citywide meeting and local church through sophisticated follow-up procedures and referral committees linking individuals with local churches, but it still remains a daunting task. Billy Graham openly admits that his style of evangelism is not the best, but defends it on the grounds that many churches are ducking their evangelistic responsibilities.

If we are to avoid the aberrations of a churchless mission (as with some evangelical mission agencies) and missionless churches that "circle the wagons," we must ensure that the *church* and *mission* are reconnected. Regrettably, there are many local congregations that simply live for themselves. They need to hear Archbishop William Temple's caution that "the Church that lives for itself will eventually die by itself." Once again we turn to *Evangelii nuntiandi* to underline the point: "[H]ow can one wish to love Christ without loving the Church, if the finest witness to Christ is that of Saint Paul: 'Christ loved the Church and sacrificed Himself for her?'" (*EN* 16)

Identification with Christ

In the Roman Catholic understanding of evangelization, the emphasis has been on propositional belief and moral obedience, rather than on establishing a personal relationship with Jesus Christ through faith. Preaching tends to be moralistic, which reinforces a sense of guilt that drives the sinner to the confessional to receive priestly absolution. Forgiveness is perceived by most traditional Catholics as mediated through the ministries of the church on the basis of acts of penance, rather than through faith in Christ and the work of the Holy Spirit to convict, to activate faith, and to produce the Christlike qualities represented by the fruit of the Spirit (Gal 5:22, 23).

In recent years, a number of Roman Catholic theologians and leaders within the Catholic charismatic renewal have placed increased emphasis on the importance of the sinner exercising faith in response to grace. Ralph Martin defines "faith" as a personal relationship of trust, surrender, and abandonment to God.[6] This personal relationship has been emphasized in recent years by a renewed interest in spiritual formation and the ancient spiritual disciplines and by the impact of the charismatic renewal. It is significant that both of these movements have bridged Catholic and Evangelical communities. The renewed interest in the spiritual disciplines of centering prayer and *lectio divina* among Evangelicals has brought them into contact with Catholic resources, rather than reengage them in the spirituality of their Puritan and holiness roots.

Evangelization flows from our identification with Christ. If this is not the case, then we are not communicating good news but simply our own ego-driven ideologies. Evangelization is the "overflow" of the abundant life in Christ. It is very difficult to get half-full Christians to overflow!

As we explore further the nature of this identification we find that our two traditions diverge at this point. Within Catholicism, and especially Latin Catholicism, the emphasis is on the suffering and death of Christ. The statues of Jesus and Mary are a study in contrasts. Jesus hangs on the cross, naked and blood-stained, knees buckled and head drooping. Mary, on the other hand, is radiant and alive, with her arms outstretched in a receptive, mediating pose.

I stood on a hilltop overlooking the city of Santiago, Chile, just outside the terminus of the funicular railway. As the crowds walked to the crown of the hill on that festive day, they came bearing flowers.

---

6. Martin, in *John Paul II*, 45.

They paused to cross themselves quickly as they passed by the crucifix. Their destination was the statue of Our Lady, huge and illuminated at night, her arms outstretched over the city. I later told a priest of my experience and the concern I felt that Mary and not Christ was the primary focus of devotion. He replied: "Eddie, I, too, have stood at that spot and wept."

And yet in times of sorrow and distress, oppressed, marginalized people can identify with the sufferings of Jesus as he hung on the cross, despised by the authorities, and seemingly abandoned by his Heavenly Father. The very idea of discipleship is associated with suffering in the word *martyr.* In our hedonistic and death-denying Western culture we cannot overlook this essential aspect of the gospel.

Holy Week is observed far more within the Catholic than the Evangelical tradition, although a growing number of Evangelicals within the liturgical tradition are observing the rich drama of the *triduum,* with a Taizé liturgy on Wednesday, a foot-washing service and Eucharist on Thursday followed by the washing of the altar and the removal of all ornaments, a service at the cross, sometimes structured around the "seven words" of Jesus, and a celebratory Saturday night Eucharist, including the baptism of adult converts. But still the greatest emphasis is placed on Easter Sunday, when the crowds come to celebrate "he is risen!" It is like walking into a concert hall for the last fifteen minutes of a symphony. Evangelicals identify more closely with an empty cross than a crucifix, when the Gospel of Christ crucified and risen to deal with the sins of the world demands both.

Evangelicals need to restore the balance expressed by the apostle Paul to the Philippians when he said: "I want to know Christ and the power of his resurrection and the sharing of his sufferings by becoming like Him in his death, if somehow I may attain the resurrection of the dead" (Phil 3:10–11). You cannot know "the power of his resurrection" without "sharing of his sufferings." To share in the sufferings of Christ is both a privilege and a spiritual gift according to Paul (see Phil 1:29). It is seldom included among the spiritual gifts listed in my tradition, and I am grateful to a Jewish Anglican priest who lost most of his family at Belsen and Auschwitz for bringing it to my attention.

The People of God as the Sacrament of Salvation

Vatican II in the *Dogmatic Constitution on the Church* and *Pastoral Constitution on the Church in the Modern World* speaks of the church as the universal sacrament of salvation, or in Edward Schillebeeckx words, "The church, then, is the universal and effective sign of the salvation of all people."[7] But the dogmatic constitution document then qualifies its statement with the recognition that the church on earth "is this only 'under shadow'—she is always in need of purification."[8]

Vatican II depicted the church as a pilgrim people—with a clear sense of direction, yet stumbling and at times wandering off course. Consequently, the church needs to be called back on to the path of obedience, and to be reassembled around its Lord to hear again the commission entrusted to it.

Proclamation by Word and Deed

Both the Catholic and liberal Protestant tradition have placed emphasis on "presence evangelism." The followers of Jesus are called to be in the world as salt and light, permeating society with their presence to restrain evil and bring the light of truth and integrity. But at some point presence leads to proclamation, for the gospel must be verbalized. Catholics typically are more hesitant than are their Evangelical brethren in grasping the opportunity to speak appropriately and clearly about their faith. The vast majority of lay persons feel ill-equipped to verbalize their deeply held beliefs.

---

7. Edward Schillebeeckx, *The Mission of the Church* (London: Sheen and Ward, 1973), 45.

8. Ibid. Cf. *Lumen gentium*, no. 8.

The church must model its communication of the gospel on
the ministry of Jesus. He taught in such a way that the common
people heard gladly. They marveled at the clarity and authority with
which he spoke. His message was accessible to ordinary people. He
both aroused their curiosity and spoke to their spiritual and economic condition. He was a tireless preacher to the crowd. His mira-
cles of healing and deliverance authenticated his teaching and
provided signs indicating the nature of the kingdom, which he came
to inaugurate. That kingdom was fully present in his person,
although ambiguously present in the community of his followers.
The kingdom is both "now" and "not yet," and we live with that tension until the consummation of all things at the end of time.

Evangelii nuntiandi affirms that "at some point the Church's
witness must become verbal, because the Gospel message is not self-
evident. It must be proclaimed, for although it may be foolishness to
those who are perishing, it is the power of God to those who are
being saved (1 Cor 1:12; cf. Rom 1:16–17)" (*EN* 22).

For that message to reach to the ends of the earth and to each
succeeding generation, every baptized Christian must become a witness who is able to give a reason for the hope that is within him or
her (1 Pet 3:15). The majority of lay persons do not fulfill this obligation, either because they identify "preaching" with the ability to
deliver a homily from the pulpit, or because they do not have an adequate vocabulary to express their experience or to explain the essence
of the gospel. In regard to the first point, perhaps we should substitute the word *communicate* for *preach* in order to express the full
range of communication styles and occasions we encounter in the
New Testament. Furthermore, we need to stress the corporate
proclamation of the gospel through the community of God's people
providing a symphony of witness. *Evangelii nuntiandi* uplifts the
apostolic mission of the whole people of God, for it is the whole
church that is both called out by God in order to be sent out by him

into all the world. This divine mission is not restricted to selected individuals represented by the missionary orders (*EN* 24).

In the ministry of Jesus, word and deed are intertwined. His deeds of mercy—healing, deliverance, the feeding of the hungry, and so on—were all signs of the kingdom. In his company, they were able to experience the present reality of the kingdom. This was especially striking when Jesus was in the company of social outcasts: the poor, the lepers, Gentiles, and tax collectors, who were considered traitors and extortioners. His presence among them demonstrated the two characteristics of the kingdom: unconditional love and a transformative relationship. People were radically changed as a consequence of being with Jesus. In continuing the ministry of Jesus, the church is both medium and message, communicating through demonstration alongside proclamation (*EN* 11, 12).

Who Needs to Be Evangelized?

Having agreed on the basic elements of the gospel, the next question is to identify those who are being addressed. Evangelization is directed to the following categories of persons:

1. *Reactivating lapsed church members.* These present a particular challenge when there is high population mobility and the dispersion of Catholic communities throughout society. Furthermore, the old Christendom culture that was so pervasive in the Western world has now crumbled "leaving a very large number of baptized people who for the most part have not formally renounced their baptism but who are indifferent to it" (*EN* 56).

2. *Engaging the passive.* As a Catholic bishop commented in the course of introducing an Alpha conference held for Roman Catholic Priests at Westminster Cathedral in London: "We have sacramentalized (for Evangelicals it is more likely to be 'socialized') people into the church, but we have not evangelized them."

Evangelii nuntiandi recognizes the challenge posed by nominal Christians who do not practice their faith (*EN* 21).[9]

3. *Facing the challenge of Christians of other traditions who consider Roman Catholics to be a legitimate target for evangelization.* This sensitive issue has been addressed in a balanced manner in the report on Roman Catholic and Pentecostal relations released in 1998.[10] It frankly recognizes the scandal of a divided witness to unbelieving, or confused and disillusioned people, and calls for mutual understanding and respect. On the one hand, proselytism was acknowledged as unethical, yet on the other hand, the document affirmed that all Christians have the right to bear witness to the gospel before all people, including other Christians (*EN* 94).

4. *Winning back disillusioned former Protestants who now profess no religion.* Roman Catholic church leaders have charged that Evangelical groups are a secularizing influence in that a significant percentage of the persons that they draw from the Catholic Church to join their ranks subsequently falls away. A doctoral study undertaken by Jorge Verala in Costa Rica evaluates this claim for that country. His findings report that the CID-Gallup survey conducted in Costa Rica in 1989 indicated that of the 8 percent who deserted the Protestant church in that year, 62 percent returned to the Catholic faith, 31 percent ceased professing any religion, 5 percent became Mormons or Jehovah's witnesses, and 1 percent became Jews.[11]

---

9. For a comprehensive treatment of nominality, see Eddie Gibbs, *In Name Only: Tackling the Problem of Nominal Christianity* (Wheaton, Ill.: Bridgepoint/Victor, 1994).

10. "Evangelization, Proselytism and Common Witness: The Report from the Fourth Phase of the International Dialogue 1990–1997 between the Roman Catholic Church and Some Classical Pentecostal Churches and Leaders," in *The Pontifical Council for Promoting Christian Unity*, 97 (1998/I–II), Vatican City.

11. Jorge Isaîas Gomez Varela, "The Costa Rican Experience: Protestant Growth and Desertion in Costa Rica: Viewed in Relation to Churches with Higher Attrition

5. Working alongside other Christian groups to address the evan-gelistic challenge presented by a secularized, post-Constantinian, neo-pagan society. In many countries, significant numbers of Roman Catholics have supported Billy Graham evangelistic campaigns, serving as counselors and establishing nurture groups to disciple Roman Catholics who have experienced a personal encounter with Christ and have committed themselves to him as Savior and Lord. The church-based Alpha courses, in which the gospel is presented and shared in small groups, is also receiving significant Roman Catholic participation. This program comes out of the Holy Trinity, Brompton Church in London, a charismatic, Evangelical Anglican congregation that has itself experienced phenomenal growth and nationwide publicity through the press and television.

6. Bearing witness to Jesus Christ among people of other reli-gions. While showing respect and esteem, we must not withhold the proclamation of Jesus Christ. "In other words, our religion effectively establishes with God an authentic and living relationship which other religions do not succeed in doing, even though they have, as it were, their arms stretched out towards heaven" (*EN* 53). This same stance was upheld by the Amsterdam Conference for Itinerant Evangelists in August 2000.

> Religious Pluralism and Evangelism. Today's evangelist is called to proclaim the Gospel in an increasingly pluralis-tic world. In this global village of competing faiths and many world religions, it is important that our evangelism be marked both by faithfulness to the Good News of Christ and humility in our delivery of it. Because God's general revelation extends to all points of creation, there may well be traces of truth, beauty and goodness in many

---

Rates, Lower Attrition Rates, and More Mobility," in *They Call Themselves Christian: Papers on Nominality Given at the International Lausanne Consultation on Nominalism*, Heather Wraight, ed. (London: Christian Research, 1999).

non-Christian belief systems. But we have no warrant for
regarding any of these as alternative Gospels or separate
roads to salvation. The only way to know God in peace,
love and joy is through the reconciling death of Jesus
Christ the risen Lord. As we share this message with others, we must do so with love and humility shunning all
arrogance, hostility and disrespect. As we enter into dialogue with adherents of other religions, we must be cour-
teous and kind. But such dialogue must not be a substitute
for proclamation. Yet because all persons are made in the
image of God, we must advocate religious liberty and
human rights for all.[12]

However, within the Roman Catholic community since
Vatican II "the council has made two fundamental statements which
are to some extent dialectically opposed. On the one hand, we have
the statement that the church is necessary to salvation and, on the
other hand, that those who are 'outside the church' not only are able
to achieve salvation, but also frequently do in fact share in it."[13]

Responses to Religious Pluralism

The churches of the West have been slow to respond to the
challenge of religious pluralism. This is due to the isolation of the
Western churches from other religious traditions through the
expanse of oceans dividing us from the rest of the world, and of a
long and sad history of confrontation with both Judaism and Islam.
The churches of the East have a very different history, being birthed
within a pluralistic context, which they have continued to engage for

---

12. *Amsterdam 2000: Proclaiming Peace and Hope for the New Millennium: A
Pictorial Report* (Minneapolis, Minn.: Billy Graham Evangelistic Association, 2001),
Appendix, 122.

13. Schillebeeckx, *The Mission of the Church*, 47.

two millennia. The same is true of many churches in the majority world (that is, Africa, Asia, Latin America, and Oceania), where from their birth as a result of missionary endeavors they have faced the challenges posed by the communities of religious faith with which they are still intimately engaged through extended family relationships. However, in their case, their responses were influenced by the teaching and church disciplines imposed by the missionaries who continued to exercise control. As these younger churches gain an independent voice, the issue of pluralism is being addressed in more culturally sensitive ways.

Within both the Roman Catholic and Evangelical traditions the issues raised by a cultural context of religious pluralism has to be addressed as a matter of some urgency. The West has experienced significant migrations of peoples from non-Christian countries since World War II. People have come from Asia, North Africa, and the Middle East in search of work while others have come as refugees. Here in the United States the boundaries of "civil religion" are being stretched to become more and more inclusive. Cross-cultural mission is no longer over the sea but across the way.

Harold Netland identifies three broad questions that need to be addressed in any attempt to develop a theology of religions:

> (1) the soteriological question of the destiny of the unevangelized; (2) a theological explanation of the phenomena of human religiosity; and (3) the missiological question of the extent to which we can adapt and build upon aspects of other religious traditions in establishing the church in various cultural contexts.[14]

---

14. Harold Netland, *Encountering Religious Pluralism: The Challenge of Christian Faith and Mission* (Downers Grove, Ill.: InterVarsity Press, 2001), 310.

Within the Evangelical tradition the focus of attention has primarily been on the first question with theologians and missiologists grappling with the issue of the eternal destiny of those who have never had a valid opportunity to hear the gospel. Through no fault of their own are such persons eternally lost, or will they be judged according to the light that they had?

Tracing the development of the debate within the Roman Catholic Church, Vatican II clearly spelled out the church's position on the necessity of Jesus for salvation in its constitution on the church, *Lumen gentium* (no. 16). "The Catholic Church believes that salvation is impossible apart from Jesus but that those who 'through no fault of their own' have never heard the Good News will be judged on the basis of the light God has given them in creation and in conscience (Rom 1:2)."[15]

Evangelicals are divided on this issue with some scholars continuing to take a hard-line position, that eternal life is dependent on an individual making a conscious decision to receive Christ as Savior and Lord.[16] Others take a more open position.[17] Within the space constraints of this chapter it is not possible to explore these issues. My purpose here is to say that both traditions are grappling with the same issues, and that the answers we give to the three questions posed by Netland will have a profound influence of how we engage

---

15. Martin, in *John Paul II*, 45.

16. Ramesh Richard, *The Population of Heaven: A Biblical Response to the Inclusivist Position on Who Will be Saved* (Chicago, Ill.: Moody Press, 1994); D. A. Carson, *The Gagging of God: Christianity Confronts Pluralism* (Grand Rapids, Mich.: Zondervan, 1996).

17. See J.N.D. Anderson, *Christianity and Comparative Religion* (Downers Grove, Ill.: InterVarsity Press, 1970), rev. ed.; Stephen Neil, *Christian Faith and Other Faiths* (InterVarsity Press, 1984); Clark Pinnock, *A Wideness in God's Mercy: The Finality of Jesus Christ in a World of Religions* (Grand Rapids, Mich.: Zondervan, 1992). For a review of the range of evangelical opinion on this issue, see Gerald R. McDermott, *Can Evangelicals Learn from World Religions? Jesus, Revelation and Religious Traditions* (InterVarsity Press, 2000).

in mission, both in terms of motivation, desired ends, and attitude. Ralph Martin's observation on recent Roman Catholic documents is also reflected in segments of the Evangelical spectrum. "We have witnessed a virtual silence on the reality of hell as a consequence of people having rejected the Gospel, not believing in it, or disobeying it."[18] It's not the silence of those who have rejected the message but the failure of the church to spell out the consequences.

Complexity of the Task

The challenge the church constantly faces is that of taking the message to people of every stratum of society and in every culture. The messenger must recognize that God's presence has preceded that of the evangelist. Witness begins with just being with people and listening, not with talking. We need to learn what God has already revealed of himself, and in what ways he has graciously dealt with people, especially in times of suffering.

Catholic and Protestant theologians have struggled to express the relationship between the gospel and culture. There are a variety of understandings regarding the relationship between Christ and culture as explored by Richard Niebuhr in his classic text *Christ and Culture*.[19] But what we have come to see with greater clarity is that the church itself is not above culture.[20] Therefore, in the task of cross-cultural evangelization we have to ask, first, how does the gospel address a certain culture; in particular, what elements does it affirm, what unrealized aspirations does it fulfill, and on what aspects does it speak in judgment? Then, we have to ask what the church

---

18. Martin, in *John Paul II*, 46.

19. Richard Niebuhr, *Christ and Culture* (New York: Harper Torchbooks, 1951).

20. Rodney Clapp comments that *Christ and Culture* "was the creature of a time when few Christians could conceive of the church as itself a culture"; *A Peculiar People: The Church as a Culture in a post-Christian Society* (Downers Grove, Ill.: InterVarsity Press, 1996), 59.

should look like within that particular cultural setting. How can both the unity and diversity of church be expressed? What elements must be held in common and what can be left to local practice?

Cultures, like ancient rock formations, have many strata. There are many painful lessons of the gospel being received simply as a veneer, but without reaching to the depths of a culture. This has occurred because of the lack of cultural understanding and sensitivity of missionaries, who simply rejected as antithetical to the gospel anything that appeared to them as strange, threatening, and "primitive." Their stance was ethnocentric, reflecting an attitude of cultural imperialism. At the other extreme was the tendency of other missionaries simply to baptize culture with the gospel, with a romantic notion of a culture being normative for a people. The gospel comes to affirm and fulfill. Contextualization becomes enculturation, with the consequence that deeper issues of the fear of demons and tribal rivalries never being addressed, with tragic consequences in the subsequent history of the church in those contexts. At this point, it must also be stressed, that enculturation is just as likely to occur in the experiences of the church in North America and Europe as in any other region of the world. We all struggle to distinguish between the treasure of the gospel, the baggage of unhealthy elements in our culture, and the trash of our ethnocentric prejudice. *Evangelii nuntiandi* urges that every effort must be made "to ensure a full evangelization of culture, or more correctly of cultures. They have to be regenerated [which entails the dying of some elements] by an encounter with the Gospel. But this encounter will not take place if the Gospel is not proclaimed" (*EN* 20).

Postscript

From an Evangelical perspective, the renewed commitment to the evangelistic task understood in terms of people being invited to acknowledge Jesus Christ as their Savior and Lord, and become members in his church has brought our two religious traditions much closer together in recent decades.[21] To the extent that we live the abundant life in Christ and translate our membership into mutually supportive and accountable relationships, and witness with both conviction and humility to that divine reality, we will demonstrate the "new evangelization." It will be new in the sense of our renewed commitment to the task as two traditions that have a great deal to share with one another to our mutual enrichment. I believe that renewal will come in the midst of our engagement in mission, for every authentic engagement in evangelization results not only in the persons coming to Christ being transformed, but in those sharing the gospel being challenged and changed by the encounter.

---

21. Avery Dulles in Ralph Martin, *John Paul II*, 26, notes that Vatican II was a watershed in the new emphasis on evangelization. "Vatican II marks an important stage in this recovery. A simple word-count indicates the profound shift in focus. Vatican I, which met in 1869–1870, used the term 'Gospel' *(evangelium)* only once and never used the terms 'evangelize' and 'evangelization.' Less than a century later, Vatican II mentioned the 'Gospel' 157 times, the verb 'evangelize' eighteen times and the noun 'evangelization' thirty-one times. When it spoke of evangelization, Vatican II generally meant the proclamation of the basic Christian message of salvation through Jesus Christ."

Chapter 8

The Ethics of Evangelization

John C. Haughey, S.J.

For the last seventeen years I have been a participant in two Vatican dialogues—thirteen with Pentecostalism and the last four with the World Evangelical Alliance. These formal conversations have sensitized me to a complex issue that needs a more careful scrutiny than most Catholics realize, the relation between evangelization and proselytism. This issue merits examination both theologically and ethically. We will begin with the theological.

Evangelization and a Theology of Mission

Both Pentecostals and Evangelicals are evangelizers with a vengeance. Catholics are usually evangelizers by exception and with reluctance. The cultural clash between these two ways of seeing the mission of the churches has generated much heat and little light. What is intended to be evangelization by one person reeks of proselytizing to another.

The Great Commission

For Christians, the mandate that triggers the activity of evangelization is the "great commission" of Matthew 28:19: "Go and make disciples of all the nations, baptizing them in the name of the Father and of the Son and of the Holy Spirit." But this mandate must be examined closely since it is so central to the motivation and sense of urgency evangelizers bring to their work. It makes a difference, first of all, that exegetes assess this "great commission" as almost certainly a Matthean composition rather than an actual event or something that came from Christ's own lips.[1] There are several arguments advanced by exegetes for holding this composition thesis. First of all, the text is unique, both within the gospel itself and because the other gospels have neither such a trinitarian formula nor such an appearance by the risen Christ. A second piece of evidence that there is a literary device in this passage is the *inclusio* that reflects back to Matthew 1:22–23 ("the virgin shall be with child...and they shall call him Emmanuel"), which is completed in this passage by "and behold I am with you all days until the end of the age" (28:20).

Two more notes about this great commission are revealing. First, the historical context of the text's fashioning. Since Matthew's gospel is addressed to Jewish Christians, it seems that it was written at a time when Jewish audiences would have already heard the understanding from their converted fellow Jews that Jesus was the long awaited Messiah. Since many had concluded that this wasn't so, it was left to the converted to turn their attention to the new fields for harvest. These would necessarily have been the Gentiles, "the nations." Hence, the great commission would have been an exhortation put on the lips of Jesus so that the communities addressed by Matthew, facing the deepening, irreparable division between the synagogue and this new sect, could now with impunity get on with the inclusion of the Gentiles in their communities. A final note: The mention of baptizing in this gospel, not hitherto alluded to, and doing so with a trinitarian formula, would have been reflective of an

---

1. See Daniel Harrington, *The Gospel of Matthew* (Collegeville, Minn.: The Liturgical Press, 1991), 414–16.

ecclesial practice that was contemporary with the writing of Matthew rather than an event and mandate of the historical Jesus.

None of the above arguments is meant to suggest that the great commission was mistaken on Matthew's part or that no evangelism should be undertaken on its basis. The point is only that it must take its place with other texts and data rather than become the sole *raison d'être* for evangelization or the foundation of a theology of mission. We could consider the manner in which Jesus approached or dealt with people, for starters. Why was he not a baptizer, for example? One of the complexities we have to face is the difference between seeking converts to the church and proclaiming the kingdom of God. Jesus' concern was with proclaiming this reign of God, clearing out the underbrush of human accretions to the Torah that had rendered so many of his hearers unfree to follow their hearts and their consciences and to respond to God's movements within their desires and aspirations. Jesus freed his hearers to hear God's call in their hearts, a call to allow God to reign in their hearts.

The profound reverence he had for "where a person was" seems telling. While he called some to follow him and they left their nets, mother, father, and so on, with others he insisted that they remain with those with whom they already consorted—like the Samaritan woman or the healed Gerasene demoniac. The latter were to share their good news of experiencing the immediacy of God with those in their own communities. Of still others he demanded silence in the matter of his identity, after he had been the occasion of their experiencing the good news of God's immediate presence to them. Granted that there are complex exegetical, historical, and christological issues with each of these instances; the only point I want to make is that Jesus himself is hardly a model of the great commission as it is ordinarily understood and acted on by many modern Christians.

There is one more element in this great commission that bears closer scrutiny for evangelizing. It has to do with the communal character of each of the *ethnē*, the "nations." If one goes back to the twenty-fifth chapter of Matthew and its eschatological vision of the coming of the "Son of Man" in glory it would appear that the final judgment will be of "nations" as nations and what they did or didn't do for and to the last, lowest, least, and left behind in their midst. If this is so, then it would suggest that evangelization must not be done without taking account of the communities or other forms of group life that will be affected by it, as well as the effect it will have on "the least of my brethren" (Matt 25:45) within or on the margins of those communities. God saves people through the mutual bonds they have with one another, according to Vatican II's *Gaudium et spes*, and this "solidarity must be constantly increased until...brought to perfection."[2] What adds to this idea is implied in this eschatological scenario that envisions peoples qua peoples, each in their distinctiveness or uniqueness, being part of the new, definitive, final creation depending on how they cared for the strays among them. In brief, there is more than one great commission! So this matter of Christ identifying with the least among us pries open a further aspect of evangelization as a commission incumbent on us. It must take its place with several other commissions if we are to be true to the gospel.

A Theology of Mission

What is necessary for a healthy evangelization is a comprehensive theology of mission or missiology. Such a missiology would have to address the issue of the theological character of faiths other than that of the evangelizer. If another faith or an interpretation of the Christian faith is seen as wholly wanting in what is salvific for the errant believer, this surely simplifies evangelizing greatly. There will then be an understandable urgency about the communication of the saving truth that "we alone have." But if the evangelizers are more modest in their

---

2. *Gaudium et spes*, no. 32, in *The Documents of Vatican II*, Walter M. Abbott, ed. (New York: America Press, 1966), 231.

presumptions about how God might be saving people who are not Christian, or who are but are not of the same mind about Christ, then their evangelization will be undertaken much more attentively to the other and with how God could be dealing with them. Certainly, Jesus of Nazareth appears to have learned this to his amazement on a number of occasions (cf. Mark 7:24–40; Matt 8:5–13). And in contemporary Christianity, newer theologies of Christian mission are beginning to develop reflections and understandings about other faiths and how they might have salvific elements, understandings that were not entertained by previous generations.

My example is from the Second Vatican Council, from its *Nostra aetate* document (1965), which began to develop a theological position on non-Christian faiths. Its radically new attitude is one of appreciation of these faiths, seeing them as possessing some of the rays of truth that enlighten countless numbers of their adherents in matters moral and spiritual. The decree exhorts members of the Catholic faith to acknowledge the religious dignity of these traditions and the effective means these faiths provide that enable people who are faithful to them to achieve an integrity by means of "the spiritual and moral goods" they supply.[3] Seeing other faiths in this light, and advocating dialogue with those who adhere to them rather than evangelization *simpliciter*, began a whole new moment in the Roman Catholic Church's self-understanding and practice, both on "the missions" and "at home."

Granted, this new openness to seeing other faiths as effective in enabling their adherents to become people of religious integrity has caused seismic upheavals within Catholicism that have taken decades to even begin to absorb. *Nostra aetate* was succeeded a decade later by further, deeper probes into the subject in Pope Paul VI's *Evangelii nuntiandi* (1975).[4] Pope Paul saw evangelization

---

3. *Nostra aetate*, no. 2, in Abbott, *Documents*, 663.

4. Paul VI, Apostolic Exhortation, *Evangelii nuntiandi* (Washington, D.C.: Publications of the U.S. Catholic Conference, 1976), no. 24.

within a whole spectrum of complex issues such as "the renewal of humanity, witness, explicit proclamation, inner adherence, entry into community, acceptance of signs, apostolic initiative" (no. 24). Each of these headings deserves unpacking, but suffice it to say that while the great commission is still very much in the mix, the other elements cited here are no less essential if evangelization is going to avoid the charge of being somehow unethical.

Roman Catholicism, like many of its counterparts in the Christian world, has become more aware of what Jesus meant when he observed that there are "other sheep who are not of this fold" (John 10:16). God's ways are not our ways and God's thoughts are not our thoughts. In other words, there seem to be many who are winding their way toward the kingdom of God independently of Christian ministry and baptism. This contention does not reject the principle on which most Christian evangelization has operated, that "outside of Christ there is no salvation." It just grants that the christological boundaries of the mystery of Christ are more permeable and the movement of God's Spirit freer than our Christian tradition had heretofore imagined. None of this denies the need for evangelization; it just calls the actors to a greater sophistication and willingness to work within the mystery of God's many ways in our world. When the only thing the evangelizer needed to know about God's ways was that the unbaptized are among the damned, the evangelizer knew too little to proceed without offense.

A second theological theme needs to surface, one that has been too little attended to in the literature on evangelization, Pope Paul VI's beautifully articulated pneumatology of missiology. This pneumatology has immediate ramifications for an ethics of evangelization. In his *Evangelii nuntiandi*, he lays out the conditions for evangelization, at the core of which is the Spirit as the principal agent operating in the evangelizers and in the evangelized. Pope Paul was impressed by the gentleness of the action of the Spirit in this evangelization, noting that the growth of the church should take

157

place only "in the consolation of the Spirit." He would say that it is the Spirit that places on the lips of the evangelizer the words that will prove effective. And it is the Spirit that predisposes the soul of the hearer to be open "to the Kingdom being proclaimed."[5]

Indeed he prioritizes the matter by noting that "while the Spirit of God has a preeminent place in the entire life of the Church, it is active above all in the mission of evangelization." The Spirit is the animating force behind an individual being impelled to proclaim the gospel as well as the cause of the word of salvation being accepted and understood. Even more surprising is the observation that the Spirit is "the goal of evangelization." It is the Spirit alone who "brings into being the new creation, the new humanity at which evangelization must aim." He goes on to comment that it is the Spirit "who produces the new unity in variety which evangelization tends to evoke in the Christian community."

These contentions and insights are quite profound and, if taken seriously, would call for an evangelization, I believe, that would be much freer about its results than we have hitherto imagined. Not only is it the case that "where the Spirit of the Lord is, there is freedom" (2 Cor 3:17), but also that where the Spirit of the Lord is operating in the activity of evangelization, the contours of the response must be open to surprise by the evangelizers. The Spirit as the author and architect of the new humanity produced by evangelization builds the people of God in ways that our earlier ecclesiologies haven't and couldn't foresee. This is really a comment about the intriguing, even bewildering difference there is between the church and the kingdom. There is, of course, a mutuality between them, but not an identity. It is this nonidentity that was not discerned until the last third of the twentieth century in Roman Catholicism that has had authorities like Paul VI make statements about the theological

---

5. The quotations in this and the next three paragraphs are taken from *Evangelii nuntiandi*, no. 75.

significance of other faiths and about the "new unity in variety" the Spirit authors within Christianity.

And, finally, it is to the Spirit that Paul VI attributes the critical, crucial "discernment of the signs of the times—God's signs—which evangelization uncovers in historical reality." Without the discernment of these signs, we are too prone to try to pour new wine into old wineskins.

Political Ramifications

Theology has a way of becoming abstract. Up to this point, I have stayed at the nonhistorical and theological level about proselytizing. There are, however, important political and historical data that have to enter into the picture in order to take a fuller view of evangelization and its ramifications on whole peoples. Two areas where these ramifications are best seen are Russia and Latin America. They are among the two most problematic regions in the world in this matter of the difference between evangelization and proselytism. They have this in common: In both cases, an already established church is complaining of being harassed or at least significantly reduced in numbers by various "evangelizing proselytizers." The result, inter alia, is enormous resentment by the leadership of the already established church, Orthodox in the former case and Roman Catholic in the latter. In Latin America, for example, according to Pedro C. Moreno of the Rutherford Institute, an organization concerned with issues of religious freedom, there are presently more Evangelicals practicing their faith in Guatemala, Brazil, and Nicaragua than there are Roman Catholics.[6] According to the Latin American Catholic Bishops Conference, there are eight thousand converts moving out of Roman Catholic churches daily to go over to

---

6. Pedro C. Moreno, "Rapture and Renewal in Latin America," *First Things*, 74 (June/July 1997), 31.

other Christian bodies, most of them Pentecostal, though this number is considered far too high by some. The image of Latin America as Catholic must be brought into a more realistic focus. Of the 85 percent who have called themselves Catholics, only 70 percent were baptized and only 15 percent are practicing their faith at present.

In Russia, on the other hand, the government, at the instigation of the Russian Orthodox Church, has, as of September 1997, banned all proselytism. Catholics and Evangelicals for different reasons are a particular target of this new law. "If fully enforced, this measure will authorize the state to expel most Catholic priests and all Catholic monastic orders from Russia, close every Catholic education institution, ban every Catholic periodical and radio program and forbid Catholics to sell books or distribute tracts."[7] Totalitarianism is certainly one solution to "proselytizing."

Using the state to do its bidding, the Russian Orthodox Church seeks to gain a new degree of control that puts religious liberty at risk. It has stymied some of the more promising initiatives that have ever developed in the field of ecumenism. A "theology of sister churches," for example, had been developing as early as 1962. In 1967, Pope Paul VI had spoken enthusiastically about this development, declaring that "after long years of disputes and differences of opinion, and through the grace of God, our Churches once more recognize each other as Sister Churches despite the difficulties which arose between us in former times."[8] Uniatism (an entering into union with the See of Rome on the part of certain communities within an Orthodox church) was admitted by Roman Catholicism to be an inadequate and outdated ecclesiology of return to Rome.[9] It is now seen as having been a wrong-headed way to bring about the kind of unity that "sister churches" could and should enjoy. Ironically, the fall of the

---

7. Lawrence Uzzell, "Negotiating from Weakness," *The Catholic World Report* (November, 1997), 19.

8. *Pro Oriente*, no. 176, p. 117.

9. Ibid., no. 10, p. 16.

Berlin Wall and the freeing of Russia and the ambient nations from the hegemony of the Soviet (so-called) Union have proven to be the undoing of these promising ecclesial weavings.

Proselytism and Ethics

Having examined some of the scriptural, theological, and political matters related to the subject, we will now inquire into the ethics of proselytizing. The terms in the dispute are not self-evident, so let me say what I take them to mean.

By proselytizing, I mean an unethical encroachment on the spiritual center of another (a person or a community). By spiritual center, I mean that matrix of meanings, beliefs, and convictions the person (or community) has put together over time. These are at the core of their soul or identity and, therefore, of their respective spiritual condition. The encroachment is unethical because it is uninvited, intrusive, and disorienting, as well as because it aims at a change in the ecclesial allegiance of those encroached upon, having negatively judged their present allegiance.

Proselytzing must be distinguished from evangelizing. Evangelizing is the communication of a religious message that is intended by the evangelizer to be seriously weighed by the potential convert. The intention is to radically affect his or her spiritual center. Presuming a respect for the otherness of the other that is lacking in cases of proselytizing, the evangelizer's message is intended to reawaken, replace, rearrange, or supplant the meanings, beliefs, or convictions the evangelized live by, such as they are. Like proselytism, evangelization is also likely to have an uprooting effect, slight or profound—hence the ethical implications of both of these forms of communication.

If it is true that one person's evangelization is another person's proselytism, it is necessary to seek a further objectivity about these differing intentions and perceptions. As with any moral or immoral act, three factors are involved: intention, object, and circumstances. Given the pejorative definition of the act of proselytism that I have already expressed above, proselytizing could never be the intention of a person with any religious integrity. And the object of the act, too, would hardly be proselytizing. But the intention to evangelize is not a sufficient guarantee that the act is moral. It will depend on whether the evangelizer's understanding of mission has been fairly and critically arrived at, or whether it reflects a history of culpable ignorance, for example, saving the evangelized from the delusions of the whore of Babylon or liberating them from the tyranny of the anti-Christ. The third component of any moral act is the circumstances in which it is performed. Evangelization, for example, can be done with full knowledge of and communication with the leaders of the local church where the evangelizing takes place. The Billy Graham Crusades are a case in point, in comparison to an evangelizing done behind the backs of the local pastors.

Further objectivity can be gained in this matter by viewing it from three different social locations.

1. *Evangelization as viewed from the side of the evangelizer.* As defined above, proselytizing could hardly be the intention of his or her action. Rather, evangelization or handing on the good news or bringing a person to Christ or witnessing to the gospel—these would be some of the legitimate intentions behind the issue being examined here.

2. *Evangelization as viewed from the recipients of the act.* They alone can say whether some degree of etiquette has been breached. If there has been some unasked-for invasion of the person's privacy in hopes of uprooting him or her from his or her present spiritual condition, we clearly are talking about a violation of the person, and therefore an unethical act of proselytizing in the pejorative sense used in this article. In some cases, however, the net result of the evangelization can be a proselyte, which in the earliest, positive

usage of that term, is a convert, a person who can end up enormously grateful for "the intrusion" into his or her life with what was heretofore unknown good news.

3. *Evangelizing viewed from the side of those who have pastoral responsibility for the "evangelized."* This is where the major issue seems to be because this is where many, maybe most of the charges about proselytizing come from. Several questions have to be dealt with by these pastoral figures. How pastorally effective have they, the pastors, been with those whom they had supposed were already "evangelized"? Have the supposedly "stolen sheep" known and been nurtured in their faith? Are the negative judgments about the alleged proselytizing shared by that portion of their "flock" that has left their pastoral care? If they have already transferred their ecclesial allegiance to the alleged perpetrators, the charges lose much of their sting. If they have not, do they share your judgment about an injustice having taken place? What is the nature of the loss the congregation has suffered by the missing party's acceptance of the message of the so-called proselytizers? This loss could be financial, or it could be a blow to the prior solidarity the congregation had known. The overall effect on the immediate culture of those who had been in a more unitary situation prior to the "encroachment" is the most serious issue, not the prestige of the denomination or the self-esteem or reputation of the deserted pastor(s). But the prior cohesiveness of the affected units like spouse, family, clan, congregation, even neighborhood cannot be the sole good cited since Christianity itself, from its inception, has broken up such units by succeeding in having its adherents leave "father and mother," and so on.

Proselytizing and Human Rights

Further objectivity can be gained by subjecting both the accusers and the accused to the test of rights, the right to religious freedom in particular. Proselytizing can be an accurate accusation, notwith-standing the intentions of the would-be evangelizer, when the right of religious freedom has been violated. The most explicit treatment involving the right of religious freedom by any church was done by the Second Vatican Council in its Declaration on Religious Freedom *(Dignitatis humanae)*. The Council in defining this right claims it as something that all people have, namely, "to be immune from coercion on the part of individuals and of social groups and of any human power, in such wise that in matters religious no one is to be forced to act in a manner contrary to his own beliefs."[10] The doc-ument does not address the issue of proselytizing as such, but any act that would encroach on the inviolability and immunity each is to enjoy would have to be counted as proselytism. In addition to the issue of the right of the individual, there is the right, by extension, of the community to be left intact without being riven by outside forces preaching "another gospel" than the one it has appropriated and that has helped it to become the community it is.

But there is a second issue that may be even more germane involving the cultures within which the evangelization takes place. In modern times, cultures are invariably pluralistic, which is a two-edged sword. The one edge of pluralism is consensual and constitu-tional, mandating that there is to be no single established church that determines the character of public life. The second edge of plu-ralism is ideological. Interpreted ideologically, pluralism deteriorates into being its own meaning system, one that would dictate to all within its pale. Its mandate is to keep to yourself whatever beliefs you have subscribed to, whatever values you hold dear, whatever convic-tions you have. It is intolerant of convictions that are personal and even more intolerant of convictions that attempt to affect public life, which is construed as needing to be free of its citizens' personal beliefs and values in order to operate efficiently.

---

10. *Dignitatis humanae*, no. 2, in Abbott, *Documents*, 679.

The Ethics of Evangelization

Obviously, this ideological meaning of pluralism would be inimical to those whose beliefs include a mission to promulgate them. This version of pluralism would consign these beliefs and the mission that accompanies them to the private lives of believers, thus leaving a meaning vacuum in public life, except, ironically, for this faith-silencing ideological pluralism itself that deems citizens good insofar as they are private about their religious convictions. But constitutional pluralism is another matter. It is not only legitimate; it is also the nonnegotiable context within which modern evangelization has to take place. To ignore this sociological context is to offend the citizenry that has ratified this "separation of church and state." Any exercise of evangelization cannot afford to snub this healthy, intentional pluralism. Respecting it creates the political and ethical boundaries, not to mention the common courtesies, necessary for pursuing Christ's mission. These boundaries are not to be breached if, in the course of evangelizing, one does not want to generate an *odium fidei*.

This context of constitutional pluralism has created a free market for different faiths and propelled the more evangelical among them to be bringers of good news to any and every citizen. The evangelizer, presumably, acts because he or she perceives an absence of beliefs in the to-be-evangelized, or a poverty of beliefs, or beliefs not acted upon, or wrong beliefs. All of these entail a judgment about another. Furthermore, they entail a judgment about the other's spiritual condition as well as which beliefs are right, wrong, and/or inadequate. But a judgment about a person's spiritual condition is always an extremely delicate issue. It will avoid the gospel prohibition of judgment (Matt 7:1: "Do not judge and you shall not be judged") only if the judgment is about their purportedly mistaken views or ignorance of religious matters and the "truths" they are seeking to live on. The only way a judgment about another's spiritual condition could be made fairly would be if the person was well known to the would-be evangelizer or willingly and freely disclosed his or her condition or need to them.

This comment, of course, applies only to micro or interpersonal evangelization. When the evangelizing context is macro, that is, a scheduled event, presumably the attending persons are free to be there or not to be there. In such situations, the stated *delicatesse* about judgment doesn't apply.

Some Applicable Principles

Without getting mired in the maze of accusations and counteraccusations about proselytism that continue to erupt, especially from the two continents mentioned above, let me close with several of the principles from Christian ethics that seem to be the most apropos in this matter of proselytizing/evangelizing. They are my own distillation of the ideas that have emerged from different ecclesial sources for the guidance of Christians in the future in their relations with one another. The most useful of these is the statement from the Catholic/Pentecostal Dialogue, *Evangelization, Proselytism and Common Witness*.[11] It is clear that evangelization requires a theology of mission and must be done according to ethical principles if there is going to be a future free of inter-Christian strife, resentment, and harsh judgment.

The first of these principles is also a commandment and the greatest of all commissions: "love one another" (John 15:12). This commission has a position of greater eminence in the gospels than the so-called great commission. It should be evident that there is no true evangelization where love is lacking, in particular, love for all

---

11. *Evangelization, Proselytism and Common Witness*, The Report From the Fourth Phase of the International Dialogue 1990–1997 Between the Roman Catholic Church and Some Classical Pentecostal Churches and Leaders, PCPCU *Information Service* 97 (1998/I–II): "Unethical conduct cited includes things such as an intellectually dishonest promotion of one's community by idealizing it; misrepresenting the beliefs of another Christian community or raising suspicions about another's sincerity; every form of coercion, manipulation, or mockery; competitive evangelization; culpable ignorance of the other's tradition"; no. 93.

the parties that would be affected by any evangelization. Where love is, the Spirit is; where the Spirit is, there is growth in Christ, not to mention growth in truth and freedom. Where the Spirit isn't, there will be an unwillingness to know the already judged party, to know the truth of the place and its ecclesial history, to know the community and what is best for it, and to foresee how it will be affected by the projected evangelization. Where the Spirit isn't, there is an unwillingness to cooperate with the leadership of the place on the one hand or, conversely, with its would-be evangelizers, on the other. Cardinal Edward Cassidy, then president of the Pontifical Council for Promoting Christian Unity, expressed this principle wryly at an informal meeting with those of us who were members of the Catholic-Pentecostal Dialogue: "The Lord has not given his evangelists a dispensation from the commandment to love one another."

A second principle is more anthropological than scriptural. Anthropologically, it seems to be endemic to the way we, as human beings, are to promote with others what we ourselves have come to understand as true and good. We commend our findings to them simply because we see that what has been good for us is good for them, too, hopefully, with a minimum of self-regard. What kind of a world would we live in if this natural process of commending the good and the true to others, as we understand these, were to cease, or worse, come to be seen as an offense against civility? Pari passu with this universal human proclivity, there is the fact that, as Vatican II declared in its Decree on the Church's Missionary Activity, "the Church is of its very nature missionary."[12] If one's faith is the pearl of great price, how could one not commend it to others? How could love of neighbor not include this kind of commending and, therefore, some degree of evangelization?

A third principle is one that has been developed by Christian bodies anxious to get past the interecclesial strife latent or patent

---

12. *Ad gentes*, no. 2, in Abbott, *Documents*, 585.

in this matter of evangelization. The principle is that of common witness: "Unity in witness and witness in unity. This is the will of Christ for his people." This is the way the 1970 document ("Common Witness and Proselytism") of the World Council of Churches' Joint Working Group (which included Roman Catholics) begins.[13] Common witness, if adopted, is an idea that would revolutionize relations between Christian denominations. Its rationale is hardly radical, since to be in Christ is already to have entered into the unity Christ gives and intends. He is that unity. Therefore, to bear witness together to his gospel is an expression of that already real unity that has begun with our having been baptized into Christ. This WCC document defines common witness as "the witness the churches, even while separated, bear together, especially by joint efforts, by manifesting before men whatever divine gifts of truth and life they already share in common" (no. 6). It goes on to indicate that "missionary action should be carried out in an ecumenical spirit which takes into consideration the priority of the announcement of the Gospel to non-Christians" (no. 28).

Among the many wise recommendations in this document, the following two stand out. First, "to avoid causes of tension between churches because of the free exercise of the right of every person to choose his or her ecclesial allegiance, and if necessary, to change it in obedience to conscience, it is vital that this free choice should be exercised in full knowledge of what is involved and, if possible, after counsel with the pastors of the two churches concerned." Second, "the church which has lost a member should...examine its conscience as to how it has done its duty of bringing the Gospel to that person," asking itself whether it might have been guilty of being simply "content that the person in question should remain a nominal and official member of (the former) community" (no. 28).

---

13. *Information Service*, 14 (1971) 18, no. 1.

A fourth principle has to do with judgment, negative judgment, of the other person or of a Christian body. It is far too easy to slide from a theological disagreement about ecclesiology, missiology, evangelization, pneumatology, or soteriology to a moral indictment of the individual or the body with whom there is the disagreement. Judgment settles the issue in the mind and exonerates one from having to listen to the already judged party. The judged party's words and actions are likely to be interpreted through a dark lens that sees them wanting in integrity. It is likely to see insincerity or self-interest, dishonesty, desire for getting or retaining power, competition, indolence about evangelization, pastoral malfeasance, and so on where there isn't sufficient evidence for any of these judgments. Labels are the cheapest form of judgment. For example, using terms such as *sect* or *rapacious wolves* or *sheep stealing* or *nominal* of a person or group's Christian faith are some of the better known instances of this. If judgments are withheld, parties at odds with one another can at least come to understand one another without necessarily having to come to an agreement. On the other hand, if judgment is operating at the threshold of a dialogue, the dialogue will never succeed. The judging party or parties will simply await the chance to unfurl the list of long-harbored grudges. Evangelization needs very few rules to follow when the denomination of those being evangelized has been judged morally bankrupt or deluded or illegitimate. Evangelizers' zeal knows no bounds — or observes the most primitive forms of etiquette — when they are winning souls, freeing them from what they consider an immoral situation.

The final two principles are interconnected: repentance and forgiveness. There is no Christian body without sin in this matter of unethical forms of evangelization. I will mention only the Catholics since, being closest to them all my life and more knowledgeable about their history, I can see clearly how they are in need of repentance. The Crusades, the forced conversion of the Teutons and the

Slavs, the Inquisition, the coarse forms of "evangelization" used in the early years of Spain's and Portugal's "Christianization" of Latin America—these are just a few historical instances of the immoral promotion of the Catholic faith. Happily, the historical beginnings of the understanding of human rights emerged from the last of these sad historical atrocities committed in the name of proclaiming the gospel or ensuring its purity. The Dominicans, Bartolomé de las Casas and Francisco de Vitoria, began to articulate for the first time the inviolable dignity of the human being qua human being and how this calls for both noninterference from others for the person to realize his or her dignity, coupled with the obligation of others, including the state, to assist in this realization.

The other side of this same principle is the need to forgive those who have defamed or coerced or denied the human right of religious freedom, either by making the profession of their faith a crime or by sundering communities with adventitious, disruptive evangelizing soirees. The list of offenses to be forgiven in this matter is endless and known only too well by all who have worked in fields where proselytizing or the accusation of proselytism has been rife. If there is a refusal to forgive the offending party, there will continue to be violence in varying degrees done to one another, often in the name of proclaiming Christ or promoting the faith. All Christians lose in this situation because a fragmented Christ is not credible to the one seeking to know whether Christ is good news or just another instance of the human problem of judgment, hostility, divisiveness, and self-interest.

In short, there are serious ethical issues in this matter of evangelization that call for the full and immediate attention of all people of goodwill, but most especially those of us who make claims about the unity of the body of the Christ that we follow. The fact that proselytism has not been a major issue for the relationships that we Christians of the main-line North American churches have with one another may be attributable to our succumbing to ideological pluralism rather than a tribute to our zeal. Our Evangelical and Pentecostal brothers and sisters are a reminder that virtue always stands in the middle between what are clearly the two extremes, on the one hand a privatized, silent faith, and, on the other, an offensive, proselytizing faith.

Chapter 9 ·

Interreligious Dialogue and Mission: Continuing Questions

John Borelli

Paul VI's 1964 encyclical on the church, *Ecclesiam suam*, served a key role in the development and acceptance of an ecclesiology by Catholic bishops at the Second Vatican Council that would provide a vision of a church with a modern, ecumenical, and interreligious mission.[1] Through this was his first encyclical, Paul VI offered a constructive understanding of the church as the people of God in dialogue with the world and especially with other religious communities. As Cardinal Avery Dulles has recently acknowledged, Paul VI's use of "the concept of dialogue in its personalist form began to figure prominently in official Catholic teaching."[2]

---

1. *Ecclesiam suam*, issued on August 6, 1964, was published by the National Catholic Welfare Conference, a predecessor of the current United States Conference of Catholic Bishops, under the title *Paths of the Church, Ecclesiam suam, First Encyclical Letter, Pope Paul VI*. Though this publication is out of print, the encyclical can be found on the Vatican Website: www.vatican.va/holy_father/paul_ vi/encyclicals.

2. Avery Dulles, *Dialogue, Truth, and Communion*, Third Annual Lecture of the Catholic Common Ground Initiative (New York: National Pastoral Life Center, 2001), 6. Curiously, Dulles does not summarize the circles of spheres of dialogue accurately in his lecture, which he notes are three: with all humanity, with all

Ecclesiam suam is thus a primary text on the connection between interreligious dialogue and mission. Such a vision of a church in dialogue would be realized in postconciliar Catholicism.

A Church in Dialogue

Paul VI did not claim to be the first pope to suggest the idea of dialogue, that is, the dialogue of salvation, as the principal means by which the church fulfills its evangelical mission, or evangelization, though he was probably the first to name it. He cited several predecessors, especially John XXIII, who he said placed "an even sharper emphasis" on the apostolic endeavor of dialogue that brings Christians "as close as possible to the experience and the understanding of the contemporary world." Pope Paul distills all these reflections on dialogue into a single sentence: "Even before converting the world, nay, in order to convert it, we must meet the world and talk to it" (no. 68).

Thus, Paul VI urged the church to develop a culture of dialogue as an essential part of its self-understanding. In that discussion in *Ecclesiam suam* are elements of Paul VI's "personalist" approach, as Dulles identifies it. The pope describes dialogue as expressive of human nature, symbolic of the divine image residing in the human person, constitutive of the nature of religion as the dialogue of salvation, and fundamental for building greater communion (no. 58 ff). He devotes several paragraphs to explaining the virtues, benefits, and goals of dialogue and then concludes that the church has the catholic mission to foster unity, love, and peace in this world (no. 94). After naming the Hebrew people, the Muslim religion, and the followers of the great Afro-Asiatic religions and then acknowledging

---

monotheists, notably Muslims and Jews, and with all Christians. The second sphere also includes "the followers of the great Afro-Asiatic religions." Dulles does underscore that the sphere of Christianity includes "intra-ecclesial dialogue."

substantial differences of attitudes between ourselves and them regarding true religion, he declares the church's respect for the moral and spiritual values of these religions and its desire to promote common ideals and to explore them through dialogue in genuine, mutual respect (nos. 107–8).

The conciliar documents that followed *Ecclesiam suam* incorporate and develop these ideas and suggestions. *Lumen gentium*, the Dogmatic Constitution on the Church, promulgated later in 1964, describes the church as "a sign and instrument, that is, of communion with God and of unity among all men" (no. 1). It states that the church has been given "the mission of proclaiming and establishing among all peoples the kingdom of Christ and of God" (no. 5). While teaching that the Church of Christ subsists in the Catholic Church (no. 8), the council recognizes that elements of sanctification and truth are found outside the visible confines of the Catholic Church. Because of this, the Catholic Church "is joined...to the baptized who are honored by the name of Christian but who do not however profess the Catholic faith in its entirety or have not preserved unity or communion under the successor of Peter" (no. 15). Furthermore, *Lumen gentium* declares that the plan of salvation includes not only the Jews, "that people to which the covenants and promises were made," but also "those who acknowledge the Creator, in the first place among whom are the Muslims" (no. 16). Jews, Muslims, and all who seek God, even those who have no explicit knowledge of God but strive to live good lives, are recipients of God's grace and may achieve salvation.

Nostra aetate, the Declaration of the Relation of the Church to Non-Christian Religions, and *Ad gentes*, the Decree on the Church's Missionary Activity, were issued in the final session of the Council in 1965. Even before Paul VI had written *Ecclesiam suam*, he stated with some feeling his desire to expand the church's attitude toward the followers of other religions in his first address to the Council soon after his election. Two paragraphs in that address are quite significant, although only a few words, conveying a somewhat negative message, would be quoted in future papal documents:

> The Catholic Church looks into the distance, beyond the confines of the Christian horizon; how could she place limits on her love, if this very love is to be that of God the Father who showers his favors upon everyone (cf. Mt 5:45), and who so loved the world that for it he gave his only Son (cf. Jn 3:16)? Look therefore beyond your own sphere and observe those other religions that uphold the meaning and the concept of God as one, Creator, provident, most high and transcendent, that worship God with acts of sincere piety and upon whose beliefs and practices the principles of moral and social life are founded.
>
> The Catholic Church unquestionably, and to its regret, perceives gaps, disparities and errors in many religious expressions as those indicated, yet she cannot fail to turn her thoughts to them as well, to remind them that the Catholic religion upholds in just regard all that which in them is true, good and human. Moreover, in order to preserve religious sentiment and the worship of God in modern culture — the duty and need of a true civilization — she is in the forefront as the most valid supporter of the rights of God over humanity.[3]

Nostra aetate conveys this same spirit of open and loving outreach to the followers of other religions. It speaks of Jews, Muslims, Hindus, Buddhists, and those of other religions that "attempt in their own ways to calm the hearts of men by outlining a program of life

---

3. *Interreligious Dialogue: The Official Teaching of the Catholic Church*, Francesco Gioia, ed. (Boston: Pauline Books & Media, 1997), 117. The documents of the Holy See pertaining to interreligious relations and dialogue and issued between 1963 and 1995 are available in English in this single volume of 694 pages.

covering doctrine, moral precepts and sacred rites" (no. 2). The document declares that for these faithfully religious persons their "manner of life and conduct, the precepts and doctrines which, although differing in many ways from her own teaching, nevertheless often reflect a ray of that truth which enlightens all men." It says, too, that the Catholic Church cannot abandon its mission and "proclaims and is duty bound to proclaim without fail, Christ who is 'the way, the truth and the life' (Jn 1:6)." Following the principles of dialogue laid out in *Ecclesiam suam*, the text urges Christians "with prudence and charity" to engage in interreligious dialogue and "while witnessing to their own faith and way of life, acknowledge, preserve and encourage the spiritual and moral truths found among non-Christians, also their social life and culture" (no. 2).

Ad gentes was promulgated five weeks after *Nostra aetate*. It, too, presented a positive view of the beliefs of the followers of other religions but from the perspective of the church's missionary activity: "So, although in ways known to himself God can lead those who, through no fault of their own, are ignorant of the Gospel, to that faith without which it is impossible to please him (Heb 11:6), the Church nevertheless, still has the obligation and also the sacred right to evangelize." This use of *to evangelize* is meant to be a specific reference to mission, for "today as always, missionary activity retains its full force and necessity" (no. 7). A broader understanding of evangelization comprised of many elements, including traditional missionary activity often summed up as proclamation, was yet to be developed.

Ad gentes states the obligation of the church to implant itself even among those who belong to other religions if the church is to offer all people the mystery of salvation and the life brought by God (no. 10). It has the necessity of proclaiming the living God and the one he has sent for the salvation of all so that non-Christians, with hearts opened by the Holy Spirit, might freely turn to the Lord who satisfies their inner hopes and infinitely surpasses them (no. 13). At the same time, *Ad gentes* urges that evangelical workers should be trained for their work in the missions "especially for dialogue with non-Christian religions and cultures" (no. 18). In the very least, there is then a creative tension between a positive view of other religions and the necessity of proclaiming the gospel to all people, even to those with whom we are in dialogue. If dialogue is a method of accomplishing the apostolic mission of the church, then missionary activity was going to have to be rethought under a larger rubric, namely, an expanded idea of evangelization that would include interreligious dialogue as a method distinct from converting people from the worship of false gods and idols to belief in the one true God.[4]

A Vision Taken Hold

Much formal interreligious activity has occurred for Catholics in the four decades since *Ecclesiam suam* and the Second Vatican Council. Today there are formal dialogues with members of various religious groups, interreligious events and visits to synagogues, mosques, and temples, annual greetings to Muslims, Buddhists, Hindus and others on special occasions, the gradual expansion of interreligious activity in church life and theological study, and considerable theological reflection on the methods and fruits of interreligious relations and dialogue. Yet tension and controversy continue to surround Catholic attempts to clarify the role of interreligious relations and dialogue within the evangelizing mission of the church.

Dominus Iesus

The intensity and breadth of responses to *Dominus Iesus*, released on September 5, 2000, by the Congregation for the Doctrine of the Faith, give pause for reflection in this regard. It is true that many reactions were due to inaccurate headlines and stories.

---

4. *Ecclesiam suam*, no. 58 ff.

Catholics themselves voiced complaints in response to mention of the text in the media or sermons. Whether or not they understood what the text attempted to teach, many Catholics did not recognize their faith, shaped as it had been by the Second Vatican Council and subsequent developments, in what they heard and read.[5]

Responses from Catholics and from leaders of other Christian communities were such that before the end of the year 2000 the pope himself on several occasions gave assurances that the Second Vatican Council's vision of ecumenical relations and interreligious relations continues to shape church teachings and to increase in significance. On September 26, 2000, the pope sent assurances through Cardinal Cassidy to Christians and followers of other religions gathered in Lisbon, under the sponsorship of the Sant'Egidio Community for the thirteenth commemoration of the 1986 World Day of Prayer for Peace in Assisi.[6] For those other Christians in Lisbon, he reaffirmed the model of convergence toward Christian unity, which he employed in his encyclical on ecumenism, *Ut unum sint*, by citing this passage: "The long history of Christians marked by many divisions seems to converge once more because it tends towards that Source of its unity which is Jesus Christ."[7] He also reminded the followers of other religions who were at the meeting in Lisbon that as a young bishop at the Second Vatican Council he had supported *Nostra aetate* and that "dialogue is also an invitation to strengthen that friendship which neither separates nor confuses."

There are other examples of Pope John Paul trying to correct any misunderstandings caused by *Dominus Iesus*. In his Angelus

---

5. For a collection of reflections on *Dominus Iesus*, see *Sic et Non: Encountering Dominus Iesus*, Stephen J. Pope and Charles Hefling, ed. (Maryknoll, N.Y.: Orbis, 2002). The text of *DI* can also be found in *Origins* 30/41 (2000), 209, 211–219.

6. Pope John Paul II's message to Cardinal Cassidy was published in *Pro Dialogo*, Pontifical Council for Interreligious Dialogue 106 (2001/1) 11–13, and in *Information Service*, Pontifical Council for Promoting Christian Unity 105 (2000/IV), 169.

7. *Ut unum sint*, no. 22, *Origins* 25/4 (June 8, 1995), 49, 51–72.

message on Sunday, October 1, 2000, the pope assured the faithful that confessing salvation in no one other than Jesus Christ "does not deny salvation to non-Christians...," nor does the teaching of the Second Vatican Council that the single church of Christ subsists in the Catholic Church "express scant regard for the other churches and ecclesial communities."[8] In the general audience of November 29, 2000, he reviewed how salvation is offered to all nations in the covenant with Noah, in the blessings on all families through Abraham, through "a certain form of faith" found among many peoples, in "the blossoming of faith into hope as evidenced by the sacred books of other religions disclosing a horizon of divine communion," and in religious experience that opens all who have it to the divine gift of charity.[9] At the general audience on December 6, 2000, he reiterated a partnership among all religious followers: "All who seek God with a sincere heart, including those who do not know Christ and his church, contribute under the influence of grace to the building of his kingdom."[10]

In analyzing the responses to *Dominus Iesus*, Peter Chirico identifies it as an event in the ecumenical movement:

> In summary, I would say that no matter how negatively one views the content and style of Dominus Iesus, a case can be made that the interactions precipitated by that statement lead towards a papacy that communicates effectively in today's world, toward a Catholic episcopacy that operates collegially with the pope, and towards a situation in which leaders of other Christian churches feel more and more at home with the Catholic Church.[11]

---

8. Excerpts of the Angelus message of October 1 were published in *Pro Dialogo* 106 (2001/1), 13–14.

9. *Pro Dialogo* 106 (2001/1), 19–20.

10. Quoted from the text published in Catholic News Service, December 6, 2000.

11. Peter Chirico, "'Dominus Iesus' as an Event," *America* (March 26, 2001), 28.

Distinct as ecumenism and interreligious relations are, symbolized by the existence of separate pontifical councils at the Holy See and with ecumenism having the special goal of full visible communion, both forms of church relations can never be completely separated. Greater communion among Christians aids the mission of the church. While Christians may agree on certain essential aspects of mission, and more specifically on proselytism,[12] they may not agree on the value of other religious traditions. Much of the same terminology is used in both ecumenical and interreligious relations although with different emphases and nuance: dialogue, unity, mutual understanding and respect, spiritual sharing and enrichment. For Catholics, however, ecumenical and interreligious dialogue arose together as priorities and nowadays "constitute a veritable vocation for the church," to use the words of John Paul II in *Ecclesia in Asia* (no. 29).[13]

The Case of Father Dupuis

The final months of 2000 also saw the examination of Jacques Dupuis's book, *Toward a Christian Theology of Religious Pluralism* by the Congregation for the Doctrine of the Faith. On September 1, a few days before the release of *Dominus Iesus*, Father Dupuis received an advance copy of the instruction, a draft of a notification about his book, and a summons to an official meeting on September 4. Dupuis has also disclosed that it was expected at the time that his notification was to be published on September 7. As it turned out, Dupuis, accompanied by his superior general and his advocate, could neither sign the notification nor agree to *Dominus Iesus* in its

---

12. See for example *Evangelization, Proselytism and Common Witness*, the Report from the Fourth Phase of the International Dialogue 1990–1997 between the Roman Catholic Church and Some Classical Pentecostal Churches and Leaders, *Information Service* 97 (1998), 38–56.

13. *Ecclesia in Asia, Origins* 29/23 (November 18, 1999), 374.

entirety.[14] A second notification, signed in December and released on February 26, 2001, observed that "the author [Dupuis] does not conceal the possibility that his hypothesis may raise as many questions as it seeks to answer." The notification declared that "his book contained notable ambiguities and difficulties on important doctrinal points which could lead a reader to erroneous or harmful opinions."[15] Dupuis was not charged with errors or heresy but with ambiguities and speculations that might lead to error.

The connection between *Dominus Iesus* and Dupuis's case is not insignificant for a study of continuing questions between mission and dialogue and for reviewing the relationship between ecumenical activity and interreligious activity. If *Dominus Iesus* is an event in ecumenism, it is also an event in interreligious relations and in the postconciliar Catholic community's reflection on itself and its mission to dialogue with the world. Dupuis is particularly significant to the topic of mission and interreligious dialogue because he served an important role in the preparation of a text of monumental significance in the Catholic Church's reflection on the relationship between mission and dialogue, *Dialogue and Proclamation*.[16] Bishop Michael Fitzgerald, secretary of the Pontifical Council for Interreligious Dialogue, in an address on April 10, 2001, at the Gregorian University, reported that the church owed Father Dupuis a "debt of gratitude for his pioneering work in this field."[17] Bishop Fitzgerald and Dupuis had worked together on *Dialogue and Proclamation*. Father Peter-Hans Kolvenbach, Jesuit superior general, has expressed

---

14. Father Dupuis gave this information in an interview with three reporters from *Indian Currents Associate News* on March 17, 2001, which was posted at the website: http://web.tiscalinet.it/icurr/ic10/interview.htm.

15. The text was published in *Origins* 30/38 (March 8, 2001), 605, 607–8.

16. *Dialogue and Proclamation* can be found in *Origins* 21/8 (July 4, 1991), 121, 123–35; also in William R. Burrows, ed., *Redemption and Dialogue* (Maryknoll, N.Y.: Orbis, 1993), 93–118.

17. Michael L. Fitzgerald, "The Pontifical Gregorian University and Interreligious Dialogue," *Pro Dialogo* 107 (2001/2), 246.

the hope that Dupuis "can continue his pioneer research in the field of interreligious dialogue," describing the book that was under investigation as "justly recognized for the seriousness of its methodological research, the richness of the scientific documentation, and the originality of its exploration…into a dogmatically fundamental area for the future of interreligious dialogue."[18]

In his book, Dupuis drew a connection between ecumenism and interreligious relations by use of an analogy between the relationship of the one church subsisting in the Catholic Church with the many churches and the relationship between the church possessing the fullness of the means of salvation and other religions:

> The recognition of the ecclesiality of non-Catholic Christian churches has opened the way for a new problematic in the search for Christian unity: unity through the "return" to the one true Church of Christ…has given way to a "global ecumenism" in search of the "recomposition" of organic unity between churches and ecclesial communities in which the mystery of the one Church willed by Christ is present and operative in different ways and degrees. In a somewhat similar manner, though *mutatis mutandis*, the "ecumenical ecumenism" of the relationship between Christianity and the other religions can no longer be viewed in terms of contradiction and opposition between realization here and stepping-stones there, much less between absoluteness on one side and only potentialities on the other.…The Catholic Church will, no doubt, continue to hold that the mystery of the Church willed by Jesus Christ "subsists" (*subsistit*) in it while it "exists" to a lesser extent in other churches. Similarly, the Christian faith will continue to imply a

---

18. Published in *Origins* 30/38 (March 8, 2001), 608–9.

"fullness" of divine manifestation and revelation in Jesus Christ not realized elsewhere with the same fullness of sacramentality. Nevertheless, in both cases, the realities involved will have to be viewed as mutually related and interdependent, constituting together the complete whole of human-divine relationships.[19]

At the conclusion to its "Commentary on the Notification" on Dupuis's book, the Congregation for the Doctrine of the Faith notes that "criticism, coming from various sources, that the general 'tone' of *Dominus Iesus* is far different from that of texts such as the encyclical letters *Redemptoris missio* and *Ut unum sint*," is unfounded because these documents have different purposes and "though not identical, are in no way contradictory." It states further that "the Declaration guarantees also that interreligious dialogue—as also the ecumenical dialogue between the Christian confessions—will develop as a 'dialogue of truth.'"[20] Now, forty years after *Ecclesiam suam* and the Second Vatican Council, certain fundamental questions regarding ecumenism, interreligious relations, and the mission of the church and their integral connection are still being vigorously debated. The two singularly important Catholic documents in that development since the Council are *Redemptoris missio* and *Ut unum sint*.[21]

Interreligious Dialogue and Mission

The relationship between interreligious dialogue and mission has been a constant theme in the writings of Pope John Paul II. In

---

19. Jacques Dupuis, *Toward a Christian Theology of Religious Pluralism* (Maryknoll, N.Y.: Orbis Books, 1997), 204. I am grateful to Father James Redington, Woodstock Theological Center, for reminding me of this passage.

20. Published in *Origins* 30/41 (March 29, 2001), 659.

21. *Redemptoris Missio*, *Origins* 31/20 (1991) 541–68; *Ut unum sint*, *Origins* 25/4 (1995), 49–72.

his first encyclical letter, *Redemptor hominis* (1979), the pope described how all Christians already have a missionary and apostolic unity that allows them "to approach all cultures, all ideological concepts, all people of good will" (no. 12).[22]

The emblematic event of John Paul's leadership in interreligious dialogue was the World Day of Prayer for Peace in Assisi in 1986. That was the first time when he invited leaders of other churches and of other religious communities to join him for a day of prayer, fasting, and pilgrimage. The event has been remembered each year with a similar interfaith gathering hosted by the Sant'Egidio Community, and it was to this gathering in 2000 in Portugal that John Paul sent assurances in light of any misapprehensions caused by *Dominus Iesus*. Another such event was held in October 1999, when over two hundred guests, representing more than twenty different religious traditions, were hosted by the Pontifical Council for Interreligious Dialogue in the Synod Hall within the Vatican. Loosely structured so that most of the work took place in small groups, the gathering produced a message and a report, drafted by a committee of participants and reviewed and approved by the assembly. This was an interreligious assembly as a preparatory event for the Great Jubilee Year. The pope closed the meeting at a candlelight service on the steps of St. Peter's basilica.[23]

In his Apostolic Letter, *Novo millennio ineunte* (2000), Pope John Paul stressed the importance of dialogue and interreligious cooperation as the basis for peace in the new millennium:

> This dialogue must continue. In the climate of increased cultural and religious pluralism which is expected to mark the society of the new millennium, it is obvious that

---

22. Published in *Origins* 8/40 (March 22, 1979), 632.

23. The documents and reports of the interreligious assembly appear in *Pro Dialogo* 103 (2000/1).

this dialogue will be especially important in establishing a sure basis for peace and warding off the dread specter of those wars of religion which have so often bloodied human history. The name of the one God must become increasingly what it is: *a name of peace and a summons to peace* (no. 55).[24]

He would cite this passage on his arrival in Syria later in the Great Jubilee Year (May 5, 2001), where he would be the first pope to visit a mosque.[25]

Another theme often mentioned by John Paul II in connection with dialogue was reiterated in *Novo millennio ineunte*. Commitment to dialogue should not cause any lapse into religious indifferentism and/or any fear of offending others while we "bear clear witness to the hope that is within us." John Paul II adds that "the Church cannot therefore forgo her missionary activity" and cites the following passage from *Dialogue and Proclamation*: "[Interreligious dialogue] cannot simply replace proclamation, but remains oriented towards proclamation" (no. 56). The link between the evangelizing mission of the church and interreligious dialogue, the role of the Holy Spirit, and the leadership of the papacy in building relationships with peoples of other faiths are the hallmarks of John Paul's vision of interreligious dialogue.[26]

Dialogue and Proclamation, subtitled *Reflections and Orientations on Interreligious Dialogue and the Proclamation of the Gospel of Jesus Christ*, was co-produced by the Pontifical Council for Interreligious Dialogue and the Congregation for the Evangelization of Peoples. It is a monumental piece just in its production. It represents a

---

24. *Origins* 30/31 (January 18, 2001), 506 (emphais mine).

25. *Origins* 31/1 (May 17, 2000), 9.

26. See my article, "John Paul II and Interreligious Dialogue" in *New Catholic Encyclopedia, Jubilee Volume: The Wojtyla Years* (Washington, D.C.: The Catholic University of America, 2001), 81–88.

further development of the theme of an earlier text issued solely by the Pontifical Council, *The Attitude of the Church toward Followers of Other Religions, Reflections and Orientations on Dialogue and Mission* (1984). It is also related to John Paul II's encyclical *Redemptoris missio*. The two texts are related thematically with an encyclical taking precedence over a statement by two Roman dicasteries. The release of *Dialogue and Proclamation* was delayed nearly six months because the encyclical, scheduled to coincide with the twenty-fifth anniversary of the Second Vatican Council's decree on missionary activity, *Ad gentes*, in December 1990, was eventually made public on January 22, 1991. *Dialogue and Proclamation* then appeared on June 20, 1991.

Jacques Dupuis, in his lengthy commentary on *Dialogue and Proclamation*, points out that the relationship among all three documents on mission, the attitude of the church toward mission and dialogue, and the relationship to mission is somewhat complex in terms of their order, development, sponsoring offices, different orientations and purposes, and approval.[27] Thus when John Paul II quotes two brief clauses from *Dialogue and Proclamation*, as he does in the final paragraphs of *Novo millennio ineunte* (no. 56), to say that interreligious dialogue "cannot simply replace proclamation, but remains oriented towards proclamation," few might realize what a highly technical observation this is in light of the development of these documents.[28] *Dialogue and Proclamation* comes last among the three texts, and it would be better to cite this entire sentence from it rather than the abbreviated thought that interreligious dialogue is oriented toward proclamation: "They [all Christians] must nevertheless always bear in mind that dialogue, as has already been said, does not constitute the whole mission of the church, that it cannot simply replace proclamation, but remains oriented towards proclamation

---

27. *Redemption and Dialogue*, 121 f.
28. *Novo millennio ineunte, Origins* 30/31 (January 18, 2001), 506.

insofar as the dynamic process of the church's evangelizing mission reaches in it its climax and its fullness" (no. 82).

Dupuis points out that the wrong impression may be left if this passage from *Dialogue and Proclamation* is cited piecemeal.[29] There is a very precise meaning here for the relationship between proclamation and dialogue, which are viewed as "two ways of carrying out the one mission of the church." As this passage in *Dialogue and Proclamation* continues, it describes how love arises in the partners imparting and receiving information about their deepest religious beliefs and bonding them together as friends and spiritual pilgrims. Christians will discover the "seeds of the Word" sown in the hearts of their partners and will respond in warmth and friendship to the positive values of their religious partners and their desire to share their religious sentiments. As Christians answer questions put to them by their partners and offer their insights, proclamation serves as a completion of dialogue in this situation of mutuality and respect for one another's traditions. Christians will also ask questions of their partners and will receive explanations. This can be an occasion when the guidance of the Spirit is perceived in the dialogue: "All, both Christians and the followers of other religious traditions, are invited by God himself to enter into the mystery of his patience, as human beings seek his light and truth" (no. 84).

The relationship between mission and dialogue is complex and hence easily misunderstood, especially by followers of other religions. They retain many negative memories of missionary activity by Christians who lacked respect for the cultures and the religions of the peoples whom they were evangelizing. Human relations have histories, and these histories engage us totally, both emotionally and rationally. The emotional results of the histories of our relations require gestures of reconciliation and time for healing. Terms such as mission, evangelism, evangelization, conversion, and witness, because of the various ways Christians have used these terms and use them today,

---

29. *Redemption and Dialogue*, 147–48.

provoke negative reactions in members of other religious communities. Just as Muslims tirelessly try to explain the meaning of *jihad,* some Christians seek to explain how evangelization likewise has a positive meaning. For many Christians, *Dialogue and Proclamation* may be a real achievement in elevating interreligious dialogue as one of the most important activities in which Christians can engage as they witness the gospel to the world and fulfill the evangelizing mission of the church. But to those of other religions, the subtlety of the relationship between evangelization and dialogue is lost.

Throughout Asia, Christians, and particularly Catholics, are a small minority among followers of other religions except in one or two instances. John Paul II's apostolic exhortation *Ecclesia in Asia* (1999), which served to conclude the Synod for Asia, addresses the topic of a church in dialogue under the subhead: "A Mission of Dialogue."[30] The pope links the new evangelization "as a call to conversion, grace and wisdom" and as "the only genuine hope for a better world and brighter future" with Paul VI's idea of a church in dialogue with the world in *Ecclesiam suam*:

> As the sacrament of the unity of all mankind, the church cannot but enter into dialogue with all peoples, in every time and place....Here efforts to engage in dialogue are directed in the first place to those who share her belief in Jesus Christ the Lord and Savior. It extends beyond the Christian world to the followers of every other religious tradition, on the basis of the religious yearnings found in every human heart. Ecumenical dialogue and interreligious dialogue constitute a veritable vocation for the church (no. 29).

This presentation in *Ecclesia in Asia* on the church in dialogue is followed by two short developments on the importance of ecumenical

---

30. *Origins* 29/23 (November 18, 1999), 373.

and interreligious dialogue, respectively. Ecumenical dialogue is vital because disunity hinders evangelization, especially in Asia where people "expect from Christians a clearer sign of unity" and "are searching for harmony and unity through their own religions and cultures" (no. 30). The emphasis in this text is on how division among Christians is a counterwitness and a great obstacle to evangelization in Asia. Addressing interreligious dialogue, John Paul II calls *Nostra aetate*, "the Magna Carta of interreligious dialogue of our times" (no. 31). Then, paraphrasing *Redemptoris missio*, he says that interreligious dialogue "is more than a way of fostering mutual knowledge and enrichment; it is part of the church's evangelizing mission, an expression of the mission *ad gentes.*" He notes that among the propositions drawn up by Asian bishops who attended the synod for Asia was the suggestion for a directory on interreligious relations. Keeping in mind that the ecumenical directory begins with a reflection on the church as communion, it is significant to note that John Paul concludes his development of interreligious dialogue by noting the close relationship between communion and dialogue as "two essential aspects of the church's mission that have their infinitely transcendent exemplar in the mystery of the Trinity, from whom all mission comes and to whom it must be directed." His final thought is for the whole people of God, that is, all Christians, to communicate the gift that is theirs in Christ to others through "proclamation and dialogue."

The inversion of the terms proclamation and dialogue is noteworthy. Throughout the 1991 document, *Dialogue and Proclamation*, dialogue and proclamation appear in that order, except for the single instance in number 82, which Dupuis has said was "surreptitiously inverted" from the text approved by the Pontifical Council for Interreligious Dialogue.[31] Why did John Paul choose to use the

---

31. Jacques Dupuis, "A Theological Commentary: Dialogue and Proclamation," in Burrows, *Redemption and Dialogue*, 147.

exception here, giving priority to proclamation in a development on interreligious dialogue? *Dialogue and Proclamation* also spoke of inter-religious dialogue as aiming at a deeper sharing of the gifts of the Spirit than just mutual understanding and respect. *Ecclesia in Asia,* coming nine years after *Redemptoris missio* and *Dialogue and Proclamation,* describes interreligious dialogue as something more than fostering mutual knowledge and enrichment; it is an expression of the mission *ad gentes.* Which is the greater result of interreligious dialogue: procla-mation of the gospel or the mutual sharing of the gifts of the Spirit?

It is no wonder that the late Archbishop Marcello Zago would say in an address at the Fall 2000 Mission Congress in Chicago: "The first challenge in today's mission is to harmonize proclamation and dia-logue."[32] Archbishop Zago had the distinct honor of having served as secretary of the Pontifical Council for Interreligious Dialogue and later as secretary of the Congregation for Evangelization of Peoples. Zago understood the importance of interreligious dialogue, calling it "more and more necessary" in today's world, "neither a fashion nor a simple tactic"; rather it is "an approach that is respectful and gradual" that "should be practiced by everyone." Employing the convergence/com-munion model that is also used in ecumenical relations, Zago identi-fied the aim of interreligious dialogue as "growing together towards the kingdom of God." Thus, Zago concluded that while proclamation is "the first duty of the church," "thanks to dialogue, especially in Asia, the closing in of the communities on themselves has been stemmed so that they can thus become visible and witness their own faith and their own religious experience."

Some Remaining Questions

The CDF declaration *Dominus Iesus* reminds Catholics that many of these questions on communion, dialogue, mission, and

---

32. "Elements of the Mission *Ad Gentes,*" *Origins* 30/21 (November 2, 2000), 334.

other issues are still with us. Its stated purpose is quite specific. The task of ongoing interreligious dialogue and theoretical study of the basis for such dialogue gives rise to new questions and new paths of research, resulting in proposals and suggestions that call for "attentive discernment." The declaration itself will not "propose solutions to questions that are matters of free theological debate." Rather, it "seeks to recall to bishops, theologians and all the Catholic faithful certain indispensable elements of Christian doctrine" and "to set forth again the doctrine of the Catholic faith in these areas, pointing out some fundamental questions that remain open to further development and refuting specific positions that are erroneous or ambiguous" (no. 3).

In his apostolic exhortation *Ecclesia in America,* under the major heading "The Path to Communion" (nos. 33–51), John Paul II addressed the communion of the Catholic Church. In the three concluding numbered paragraphs of that chapter, he specifically talks about "elements of communion with other Christian churches and ecclesial communities" as well as "the Church's relations with Jewish communities" and "non-Christian religions." *Ecclesia in America* concluded the Synod for America.[33] These paragraphs mentioning ecumenism, Jewish relations, and interreligious relations are quite brief for relations as significant as these are in North America, with the largest Jewish population in the world, a complex array of ecumenical relations that have a major impact on worldwide progress toward full communion, and an increasingly influential multireligious population. The chapter, "The Path to Communion," is followed by a final chapter entitled, "The Path to Solidarity" (nos. 52–74). It is curious that Jewish relations and interreligious relations are covered in the chapter on communion, a word usually reserved for the unity of Christians. John Paul indeed recalls in *Ecclesia in America* that "the history of salvation

---

33. *Ecclesia in America, Origins* 28/33 (1999), 565–92.

makes clear our special relationship with the Jewish people" (no. 50). Thus, Jewish relations are handled carefully, without disconnecting them from ecumenical relations. Finally, John Paul restates the intention of Catholics in interreligious dialogue "to emphasize elements of truth wherever they are to be found" (no. 51). Although he describes solidarity as one of the fruits of communion, the pope did not place interreligious relations in the chapter on solidarity.[34]

At his November 29, 2000, audience, John Paul said that the religious texts of other religions "disclose a horizon of divine communion, point to a goal of purification and salvation for history, encourage the search for truth and defend the values of life, holiness, justice, peace and freedom."[35] *Dominus Iesus* seems to agree on the divine origin of these elements when it quotes *Nostra aetate* about the teachings of other religions reflecting a ray of that Truth *(radium illius Veritatis)*, which enlightens all men, and then refers to the ways in *Redemptoris missio* that God makes himself present through other religions as elements of goodness and grace *(bonitatis et gratiae elementa)* (no. 55). Indeed, it argues that the sacred texts of other religions "may be de facto instruments by which countless people throughout the centuries have been and still are able today to nourish and maintain their life relationship with God" (no. 8). If so, these writings, as well as other elements in other religions, would have in some way a divine origin providing a means for participating in divine communion.

When *Dominus Iesus* addresses the prayers and rituals of other religions, it seems to offer another judgment; it states "that one

---

34. The author has explored this observation further in his "John Paul II: *Ecclesia in America,* Diversity in Communion and Communion in Diversity," in *Milestones in Interreligious Dialogue: Essays in Honor of Francis Cardinal Arinze: A Seventieth Birthday Boquet,* edited by Chidi Denis Isizoh (Rome: Ceedee Publications, 2002, pp. 268–80.

35. Quoted in *Pro Dialogo* 106 (2001/1), 20.

cannot attribute to these…a divine origin or an *ex opere operato* salvific efficacy, which is proper to the Christian sacraments" (no. 21). This could be explained by the fact that the Latin text has no articles, and in this case it would follow from what has been said previously in the text that a definite article rather than an indefinite article is called for in the English translation. Hence, these prayers and rituals, like the writings of other religions, their teachings, and other spiritual means, do not have the unique divine origin or salvific efficacy we attribute to the sacraments and the inspired writings of the Bible. This does not mean that they do not have a divine origin and a certain salvific efficacy.

Jews do not have the sacraments either, but they do have the covenant with God. For Cardinal Walter Kasper, this seems to have salvific efficacy. In May 2001, he assured his Jewish partners in dialogue at a meeting of the International Catholic-Jewish Liaison Committee that "the church believes that Judaism, i.e., the faithful response of the Jewish people to God's irrevocable covenant, is salvific for them, because God is faithful to his promises." Furthermore, the cardinal assured Jewish participants that "mission…cannot be used with regard to Jews, who believe in the true and one God." He was using the term mission "in its proper sense," which "refers to conversion from false gods and idols to the true and one God, who revealed himself in salvation history with his elected people."[36]

In an earlier reflection on religious diversity addressed in October 2000 to an international missionary congress meeting in Rome, Kasper spoke of faith in the unity and unicity of God as something that "unites Judaism, Christianity and Islam, and distinguishes these three monotheistic religions from all other reli-

---

36. Cardinal Kasper's communication to Jewish representatives was entitled "*Dominus Iesus*" and was published under the title, "The Good Olive Tree," *America* 185 (September 17, 2001), 14.

gions."[37] It is also true that each of these traditions understands the unity and unicity of God. Nevertheless, if Jews, Christians, and Muslims believe this, then their act of faith is a response to the grace of the one God revealing his presence to them. *Dominus Iesus* defines faith as "the proper response to God's revelation" and as "a gift of grace" (no. 7). The declaration also suggests a distinction between theological faith, which is the acceptance in grace of revealed truth, and belief, which in the other religions is the sum of experience and thought in the search for truth, a distinction it says must be firmly held (no. 7). Avery Dulles has called this distinction "somewhat problematical." He cites the passage from the Second Vatican Council's *Ad gentes* (no. 7), citing Hebrews 11:6 to the effect that God makes it possible for persons ignorant of the gospel to attain "that faith without which it is impossible to please him."[38]

Conclusion

The Second Vatican Council ushered in a new era for Catholics with important implications for evangelization. The theological basis for this was an understanding of the church in dialogue, with implications for missionary activity, ecumenism, and interreligious relations, first documented in Paul VI's encyclical on the church, *Ecclesiam suam*. This understanding of the church was further developed in the documents of the Second Vatican Council.

---

37. Walter Kasper, "Relating Christ's Universality to Interreligious Dialogue," *Origins* 30/21 (November 2, 2000), 326. The USCCB's Committee for Ecumenical and Interreligious Affairs' dialogue with the National Council of Synagogues has issued a document that draws considerably from Cardinal Kasper's remarks on mission and the Jews. See "Reflections on Covenant and Mission," *Origins* 32/13 (September 5, 2002), 218–24.

38. Avery Dulles, "A Symposium on the Declaration *Dominus Jesus*," *Pro Ecclesia* 10/1 (Winter 2001), 5.

Lumen gentium and *Unitatis redintegratio,* using a theology of the church as a communion of the faithful, identified a real but imperfect communion existing among all Christians and expressed the prayer and hope that unity will be achieved through ecumenical dialogue, so that the light of the gospel will shine more brightly. *Nostra aetate* and *Ad gentes* encouraged interreligious dialogue so that Christians witnessing to their faith might acknowledge and preserve what is true and good among the religious beliefs and practices of others. In all of these documents, Christians are urged to carry out the mission of the church through dialogue and proclamation. Particularly new in these documents is a spirit of openness, respect, and admiration for the spiritual riches of other religious traditions, fostered by Paul VI and dramatically evident in the pontificate of John Paul II.

The Pontifical Council for Interreligious Dialogue and the Congregation for the Evangelization of Peoples addressed together the relationship between dialogue and proclamation within the evangelizing mission of the church in the jointly prepared text, *Dialogue and Proclamation.* Jacques Dupuis, who assisted in the preparation of the text, has observed that a certain tension between dialogue and proclamation remains in the text because it was "subject to two distinct influences."[39] One view was to see interreligious dialogue as an authentic form of evangelization; the other was to present evangelization as always entailing a clear proclamation of Jesus Christ, which is the central element without which all the other elements of evangelization lose cohesion and vitality. Proclamation as such is not always present in an interreligious dialogue although the Christian participants witness to the gospel by their presence and contributions to the conversation. If proclamation is the central element of evangelization (no. 76), are those occasions when dialogue does not involve actual instances of

---

39. Dupuis, "A Theological Commentary," in Burrows, *Redemption and Dialogue,* 154.

proclamation genuine forms of evangelization? Dialogue is called "an integral element" of evangelization and proclamation (nos. 9, 38), the "foundation, core and summit" without which the other elements lose their cohesion and vitality (nos. 10, 75, 76). *Dialogue and Proclamation* concludes with the observation that dialogue remains permanently oriented toward proclamation, which is the achievement of the climax and fullness of the church's mission (no. 82).

The encyclical *Redemptoris missio,* immediately preceding *Dialogue and Proclamation,* gave a "permanent" priority to proclamation (no. 44). It is also the most authoritative Catholic text since the Second Vatican Council's *Nostra aetate* to say something about interreligious relations. In the section on the Holy Spirit, the principal agent of mission, John Paul II, introduced his personal reflections on the 1986 World Day of Prayer for Peace: "Excluding any mistaken interpretation, the interreligious meeting held in Assisi was meant to confirm my conviction that 'every authentic prayer is prompted by the Holy Spirit, who is mysteriously present in every human heart'" (no. 29).

He also introduces the strongest endorsement in an important document of the church for interreligious dialogue by observing that such dialogue is both a part of the church's evangelizing mission and not "in opposition to the mission *ad gentes;* indeed it has special links with that mission and is one of its expressions" (no. 55). While he says that this mission "is addressed to those who do not know Christ and his Gospel, and who belong for the most part to other religions," he also offers a positive assessment of the religions themselves: "[God] does not fail to make himself present in many ways, not only to individuals but also to entire peoples through their spiritual riches, of which their religions are the main and essential expression even when they contain 'gaps, insufficiencies and errors'"(no. 55). The words, *gaps, insufficiencies and errors,* are indeed taken from Paul VI's 1963 address to the Second Vatican Council, but the intention of the passage was to promote a positive attitude "that the Catholic religion upholds in just regard all that which in them is true, good and human."[40]

A certain tension remains within *Redemptoris missio*. While John Paul II expressed joy that the Holy Spirit works in the hearts of all individuals when they turn toward the things of God and affirmed the religious expressions of peoples outside the church as among the means through which God reveals himself to people of other religions, he asserts that there is "no conflict between pro-claiming Christ and engaging in interreligious dialogue" (no. 55). Here he cites a 1990 letter to the bishops of Asia: "The fact that the followers of other religions can receive God's grace and be saved by Christ apart from the ordinary means which he has established does not thereby cancel the call to faith and baptism which God wills for all people."[41]

After the release of *Dominus Iesus*, it became apparent that the tension between interreligious dialogue and mission is still widely felt, particularly in Christian-Jewish relations. Jews, for whom the covenant with God remains intact, represent a special case. A doc-trine of evangelization broadly directed at everyone, including a "new evangelization" (*Redemptoris missio*, no. 33) directed at Christians themselves, still prompts Jews to ask if there is a mission directed at them. Is the covenant with the Jews a part of the ordinary means of salvation? Does a Christian desire for all to come to faith and baptism apply also to Jews? Are the attitudes and approaches that various Christians hold and take toward the followers of other reli-gions among the church dividing issues?

Finally, the tension between dialogue and mission is felt by those engaged in interreligious dialogue. After all, as Cardinal Kasper has said: "For us, interreligious dialogue is not a one-way street; it is a true encounter that can be an enrichment for us

---

40. *Interreligious Dialogue*, 117.
41. Ibid., 437.

Christians."[42] By affirming, respecting, and defending everything in other religions that is true, good, noble, and holy, Christians should not let pass whatever they believe is detrimental to the honor of God and human dignity, nor do they forfeit their right to invite others to faith in Jesus Christ.

There are indeed those occasions in interreligious dialogue when Christians also learn and receive criticisms and invitations. If interreligious dialogue has a rightful place in the dialogue of salvation originating from God and offered to all humanity, God is honored and served by a dialogue of love forming the spiritual bonds among the participants. Thus, a certain tension will always remain between having a complete openness to others in dialogue and expressing one's most profound feelings and beliefs. As Christians seek language to explain this relationship between dialogue and mission, they also know that they are exploring areas of human relations that are largely uncharted. Theological judgment must be open to renewal as more and more lessons are learned.

---

42. "Relating Christ's Universality to Interreligious Dialogue," *Origins* 30/21 (November 2, 2000), 327.

List of Contributors

LAURA NIEMANN ANZILOTTI, after graduating from the University of Notre Dame, coordinated a number of service learning programs at the university's Center for Social Concerns and spent a year in a volunteer program in San Juan, Puerto Rico. She has done graduate work in theology and is presently involved in youth ministry at St. Francis Xavier College Church in St. Louis. She has three children.

JOHN BORELLI is the special assistant to the president for interreligious activities at Georgetown University; previously he was the associate director of the Secretariat for Ecumenical and Interreligious Affairs of the U.S. Conference of Catholic Bishops. Since 1990 he has been a counsultor to the Vatican's Pontifical Council for Interreligious Dialogue.

WILLIAM R. BURROWS is managing editor of Orbis Books, Maryknoll, New York. A former member of the Divine Word Missionaries (SVD), Burrows worked from 1972 to 1977 teaching theology in Papua New Guinea. He taught at Catholic Theological Union in Chicago and lived and worked in an African American parish on Chicago's far south side.

ALLAN FIGUEROA DECK, S.J., is president of the Loyola Institute for Spirituality in Orange, California. Father Deck has lectured and written widely on Hispanic ministry, popular Catholicism, faith and culture, and Catholic social teaching. He is a co-founder and first president of the Academy of Catholic Hispanic Theologians of the United States and of the National Catholic Council for Hispanic Ministry.

AVERY CARDINAL DULLES, S.J., is the Laurence J. McGinley Professor of Religion and Society at Fordham University, Bronx, New York. The author of twenty-one books and seven hundred articles, he is a past president of the Catholic Theological Society of America and served on the International Theological Commission in Rome. Created a cardinal by Pope John Paul II in 2001, he is the first American-born theologian who is not a bishop to become a cardinal.

EDDIE GIBBS is an Anglican priest from England. After serving in a London parish, he spent the next twelve years with the South American Missionary Society, first in Chile and then on the U.K.-based staff. Since 1984, he has been on the faculty in the School of World Mission at Fuller Theological Seminary in Pasadena, California, where he is currently the Donald A. McGavran Professor of Church Growth.

JOHN C. HAUGHEY, S.J., has been professor of Christian ethics at Loyola University of Chicago's graduate program since 1991. He was appointed by the Vatican's Pontifical Council for Promoting Christian Unity to the Dialogue Between the Roman Catholic Church and Some Classical Pentecostal Churches and Leaders (1985–1998); in 1999 he was appointed to the Roman Catholic/World Evangelical Alliance Consultation. He has published numerous articles and ten books.

THOMAS P. RAUSCH, S.J., is the T. Marie Chilton Professor of Catholic Theology at Loyola Marymount University in Los Angeles. A specialist in the areas of ecclesiology and ecumenism, he has published ten books and numerous articles. He is a member of the Roman Catholic/World Evangelical Alliance Consultation and co-chairs the Catholic/Evangelical Committee in Los Angeles.

List of Contributors

ROBERT S. RIVERS, C.S.P., is the director of Diocesan and Parish Services for the Paulist National Catholic Evangelization Association. Father Rivers served as a campus minister at state universities in Minnesota and Texas and as pastor of Paulist parishes in Greensboro, North Carolina, and Los Angeles, California. He specializes in preaching and teaching in order to assist dioceses and parishes to carry out the saving mission of Jesus Christ.